The
FLAVOR
of
OUR FAITH

DOUBLEDAY

NEW YORK · LONDON · TORONTO · SYDNEY · AUCKLAND

The

FLAVOR

of

OUR FAITH

*Reflections on Hispanic Life
and Christian Faith*

✝

KAREN VALENTIN

with

REVEREND EDWIN AYMAT

PUBLISHED BY DOUBLEDAY
a division of Random House, Inc.

DOUBLEDAY and the portrayal of an anchor with a dolphin are
registered trademarks of Random House, Inc.

Book design by Amanda Dewey

Library of Congress Cataloging-in-Publication Data
Valentin, Karen.
The flavor of our faith : reflections on Hispanic life and Christian faith
= El sabor de nuestra fe / Karen Valentin.— 1st ed.
p.   cm.
In English.
1. Hispanic Americans—Prayer-books and devotions—English.
I. Title: Sabor de nuestra fe. II. Title.
BR563.H57V35 2004
277.3'083'08968—dc22   2004047784

ISBN 0-385-51076-4

PRINTED IN THE UNITED STATES OF AMERICA

November 2005
First Edition

1   3   5   7   9   10   8   6   4   2

I dedicate this book to Mami, Papi, and Alela.
There would be nothing to write without your love.

CONTENTS

ACKNOWLEDGMENTS

Special thanks to Adrienne Ingrum, who envisioned this book and entrusted it to me. I am grateful for your friendship, encouragement, prayers, and advice.

With great love and appreciation to my family and friends: Thank you for sharing your wonderful stories.

Many thanks to Michelle Rapkin and Frances O'Connor for giving me the opportunity to fulfill a dream, and for all the wonderful suggestions that enrich this book.

INTRODUCTION

The *Flavor of Our Faith* is an armchair journey for both Hispanics and non-Hispanics alike. The destination is a deeper relationship with Christ via a path of cultural awareness, appreciation, and connection. Scriptures and prayers accompany the reflections and tie in the various spiritual metaphors addressed in each story. They are designed so that you may tailor them to your own conversations with God.

These reflections are based on my own experiences and stories from family and friends. Growing up in a Hispanic and Christian household seasoned my life with a distinct flavor, yet I often felt disconnected from those identities. It was as if my family had the ingredients to be genuine, but all I could do was enjoy the feast they prepared. I heard Spanish being spoken all around me, but I spoke only English. I saw my family's love for Christ, but my understanding was too vague to share the same passion. This book is a collection of experiences and realizations that helped me come to know Christ in a deeper way and embrace my culture as my own.

The ingredients that make up *The Flavor of Our Faith* are issues culled from several generations and various perspectives. Unlike a meal presented on a neat platter, it is not one seamless story. As you read and discover the taste of each story, you must be the one to combine the elements that speak to you and blend those flavors to reach your own conclusions.

The making of the book was an intergenerational effort. While the reflections are from my youthful perspective, my maternal uncle, the Reverend Edwin Aymat, played a crucial role in creating *The Flavor of Our Faith.* He brought his broad experience and wisdom to this book, wrote many of the beautiful prayers, and selected relevant Scriptures to accompany each chapter. He has been an ordained minister for thirty-five years and serves as pastor of a bilingual ministry. He has held various offices in Hispanic Christian leadership groups, and his advice and counsel—as I wrote and sought feedback—proved indispensable.

While I address Latin issues and experiences, I hope non-Hispanics will read each story as welcomed guests into this world. Hispanics are rapidly becoming the largest ethnic group in the United States; however, we have been weighed down in our society by negative depictions, stereotypes, and narrow representations. They present the bitter without exploring the true flavor. The same can be said for the portrayal of Christianity. This book presents a wide array of issues concerning both Hispanic culture and Christianity and explores how they clash or blend with American traditions. Regardless of your cultural background, I pray you will connect with God through each and every piece.

I invite you to this feast of reflections, and whether the taste is familiar and reaffirming or exotic and new, I hope *The Flavor of Our Faith* helps you "Taste and see that the LORD is Good" (PSALM 34:8, NEW INTERNATIONAL VERSION).

The

FLAVOR

of

OUR FAITH

SHRINE OF RICE AND BEANS

There is a time for everything, and a season for every activity
under heaven: a time to be born and a time to die,
a time to plant and a time to uproot . . .

ECCLESIASTES 3:1–2

WHEN MY GRANDMOTHER suffered a stroke, we moved her things for the second time. We slowly filled boxes with quilts, pots and pans, picture frames, and broken music boxes. These familiar old objects had done their best to make this suburban residence her home. Yet ever since we had moved these very treasures in five years before, they had always seemed like orphaned children in a strange land.

"Remember this?" my mother asked that day, extending a small photo album. I smiled at the black-and-white photos I had taken days before my grandmother moved from her small Brooklyn apartment. I flipped through the album and smiled at pictures that might have seemed strange to anyone else—a doorbell, a stove, a fire escape, a kitchen sink.

The day I took those pictures, my grandmother, as always, had been waiting by the window. It was an image I could always count on when I went over for a visit. She blew me a kiss as I tilted my head back and captured my first picture of the day. I took another photo of the vertical row of doorbells, and one of the long staircase that led to her second-floor apartment. When I reached the open door, I gave Alela a tight hug and a loud kiss on the cheek.

"Did you eat?" she asked, walking over to the stove to stir the rice.

"I'm not hungry," I responded, looking at the cardboard boxes packed and ready to go. Alela lowered the flame and walked to the bedroom, leaving me alone in the kitchen. I held the camera to my face and took several pictures of the ancient stove, a shrine of rice and beans.

The table nearby was empty, but I could picture members of my family in every chair, talking, laughing, and eating her delicious food. With the scent of the food in the air and these memories in my mind, I regained my appetite and filled a plate with white rice, pink beans, and roasted chicken. I ate every bite at the quiet table, then washed my dish in the tall, deep sink, where, until I was about eleven, I had needed to climb onto a chair to wash my hands.

Camera in hand, I climbed through the kitchen window onto the bright yellow fire escape, where Alela's plants sat contentedly in the sun. When I was a little girl, she would let me sit out there on a folded blanket and would serve my lunch on the windowsill. The thin white curtains would sway back and forth in the breeze, as if dancing to the distant rhythm of salsa. Peering through the yellow bars, I looked down at the landlord's backyard, with the picnic table that no one ever seemed to use.

I continued to wander around the apartment, packing away memories inside my little black camera until the film ran out.

As I left that day, I hugged Alela good-bye and, as usual, promised to look both ways before crossing the street, to keep my eyes open for *locos*,* and to stand away from the edge of the subway platform. Once outside, I looked up at the window where I knew she'd be. "I love you!" I shouted, blowing kisses as I walked away. At the end of the block, I turned, to see her still leaning out of the window and waving until I turned the corner.

Sitting with my mother, I closed the picture album and put it in the cardboard box with the other things I wanted to keep.

One month later, my grandmother died in her hospital bed. I can no longer hold her, or taste her wonderful food, but the abundance of her love and the treasure of memories will always remain.

Prayer

Thank you for special people who have filled my childhood with a feast of memories. The love they've shared will continue to live beyond the number of their days. Help me to be the kind of person who will be remembered by others when I'm called to be with you.

---

* Spanish words and expressions throughout this book are defined in the Glossary on page 157.

NUYORICAN SPANISH

I can do everything through him who gives me strength.

PHILIPPIANS 4:13

"V AMOS A HABLAR *Español.*" Every now and then, I'll announce
this to my parents, insisting we speak in Spanish only! I'm
determined when I say this, but we're always back to English
within the hour. For me, speaking Spanish is like some kind of
floating device you pull underwater. Once you let it go, it shoots
right back up to the surface of English, where it feels natural.

I understand Spanish perfectly. I grew up with it spoken all
around me. It was spoken among my family, at my church, and in the
novellas Alela watched on the Telemundo Network. So why does it
feel like I have a mouthful of marshmallows when I try to speak? It's
the story of the Nuyorican, one many like me can relate to.

When I was growing up, my parents and extended family con-
versed with one another in Spanish. Yet they spoke to us kids in

English—even my father and grandparents who had thick Spanish accents. My mother feared learning the two languages would confuse us children, and she assumed we'd pick up Spanish eventually. I did pick it up, but only random words, like a collection of pretty beads—*casa, pollo, gracias, mira.* The problem was, I never learned to string them together and make a decent sentence.

As I grew older, I had a desire to learn, but with it came greater frustration and embarrassment. I could almost feel the burn of stares as I stuttered out harsh, jagged words, stabbing the language to death. People smiled and helped me along with verb tenses and pronunciation, but I know perfectly well they were thinking, What kind of Hispanic are you?

When I started to learn French, the experience was completely different and refreshing. There was no weight of "You should know this by now." I enjoyed learning so much that before I knew it, I was flowing better in French than in Spanish. I felt like a bit of a traitor, but I also had a new sense of confidence. If I could learn French from scratch, there was no reason I couldn't learn a language that I had been hearing all my life. I also realized what had been stopping me. I knew I had to shake off the terrible weight of shame that had been keeping me from enjoying a language dear to my heart. I know that in the future, with a little work, my collection of words will no longer be scattered on the floor. I'll string them together with slow determination, until I can finally wear them with pride.

Prayer

Lord, help me accomplish the things in life that seem intimidating and difficult. I know I can do anything as long as you're guiding me and giving me strength in the process.

TREASURES IN THE SAND

✛

They will summon peoples to the mountain and there
offer sacrifices of righteousness, they will feast on the abundance
of the seas, on the treasures hidden in the sand.

DEUTERONOMY 33:19

A FTER I FINISHED teaching a gymnastics class one day, a student and her mother approached me with a request. "Would you like to be a mother's helper this summer?"

My initial thought was "I don't think so!" but I smiled politely and let them finish. As they did, my smile grew wider, and so did my excitement over the proposal. They owned a house just steps from the beach on Fire Island. My job would be to stay with the girls while their parents worked and remained in the city.

"The girls are old enough to do their own thing, so the days are pretty much your own," the mother continued, trying to sell the idea. But I was already sold. "Sure, I'll do it. I'd love to!" My head filled with images of an incredible paid vacation. All I really had to do was walk the dog, keep the house tidy, and cook for the girls.

I could barely contain myself on the ferry ride to the island. I squeezed in with the rest of the crowd near the exit as the boat slowly settled into the harbor. The crowd was a mix of Hispanics, whites, and African Americans. I was too excited to notice that the only family groups were white. As I settled into the beach house, I finally realized, Oh, we're the hired help. Having grown up in the city, shuffled in with other races and social classes, I was unprepared for the sharp dividing line of minority servants on one side and rich white families on the other. I was greatly bothered by the fact that mostly Hispanic and African American women were the ones pushing strollers five paces behind mothers in tennis outfits, lingering behind like shadows.

While I was thankful that my days weren't spent that way, the house was huge and took much time to clean. There was laundry to do every day, and the big dog I had to walk three times a day intimidated me. The hours left to myself were lonely and boring.

When the girls' parents were there—Thursday nights through Sunday nights—I'd feel awkward and out of place. I didn't feel free to socialize with them or their weekend guests, so I kept to myself. I was their "help." The deep tilt in the social and racial scale had a profound effect on me. In one short month, I felt insecure, jealous, and even prejudiced. My emotions were as turbulent as the waves I heard every day.

One morning, I rose early and took a walk on the beach. The waves were calm and the sun was shining brightly. The sand was sprinkled with shells and rocks of all shapes and colors, reflected in the rays of the morning sun. They looked like rare and precious jewels laid out just for me. I began to collect them as the soft waves washed my feet with a gentle touch. I looked at the treasures in my hand and felt the presence of God ministering to my heart. I looked at the sparkling ocean that seemed to have no end and thought of God's everlasting love and abundant gifts. A gentle peace washed over me, and the bitterness and insecurities seemed to drift away toward the horizon. With each rock and shell I lifted from the sand, I counted my blessings and thanked God for priceless treasures only He can give.

Prayer

Lord, like the variety of treasures you have scattered on the shores, you've created me with special care. Thank you for revealing that my true worth is not measured by the standards of this world. In times of insecurity, help me to remember that I am the child of a King.

ENGRAVED

As you come to him, the living Stone—rejected by men but chosen by God and precious to him—you also, like living stones, are being built into a spiritual house to be a holy priesthood . . .

1 PETER 2:4–5

WE CLIMBED over the thick white tombs in Puerto Rico as if they were ancient hills waiting to be discovered. Tropical flowers adorned the all-white cemetery, which was packed with statues and large cement vaults with marble covers. I stepped up and down from box to box, searching for my grandfather's name, despite my father's insistence that I'd never find it. "We buried him in the dirt," he repeated. "We had no money for a stone." I continued in search of a marker or a sign—something with his name on it. Among the tight clusters of marble and stone, we found a few patches of dirt, but the simple crosses pressed into the soil bore other names.

Finally convinced that they had covered his site with another, I shrugged off my defeat and prepared to leave. Yet when I turned to call my father, he was standing among the statues like a lost child. I knew his thoughts as he stood there alone. He had returned to the days of bare feet, long walks to school, and the little wooden house with a roof of sugarcane leaves. I also recalled those stories, and with images no longer vague, I walked beside him in my mind.

I observed a man I never knew return home with a large bundle of wood on his shoulders. It was the same bundle he'd left with in the morning, hoping to sell it. He threw the heavy sack of wood on the ground and, on his hands and knees, wept over the scattered pieces. My grandmother, young and beautiful, consoled her husband, easing him into the house to drink cofffee. Seeing the wood left on the soil, I thought of the two children they would soon bury.

My grandfather worked even harder after the death of his children, always looking for a way to earn money. He constructed a stove in the back of their home with large heavy stones, and sold cakes and loaves of bread for a penny each. As he worked to feed his remaining family, he encouraged my father to work hard in school. "When you graduate sixth grade, I'm going to buy you a pen," he promised. He died before he could see his son graduate and offer him the promised gift.

The discipline of hard work was passed to my father. After high school, he cut sugarcane, sold wood, helped his mother cook, and looked after his brother and sister. As a man, he continued to work hard so that his own children would never understand the meaning of hunger.

The poverty of his past, which had taken away so much, returned to take one last thing. Surrounded by stone memorials meant for other families to see, my father stood there with nothing.

"He was a good father," he said as he noticed me sitting quietly nearby. "He worked hard all his life to take care of us."

I looked at this living memorial and realized that my father was my grandfather's stone. The life and death of his father were not only engraved in his memory but have formed him into the man he now was—a good father, a hard worker, a wonderful cook, a money saver, a man who had returned to school when he finally had the time, and who had graduated from seminary at the age of fifty-eight. I wished I had thought of my grandfather's promise when my father marched down the aisle wearing his cap and gown. I would have bought him a beautiful pen.

Prayer

Lord, please make my life be a witness to who you are and what you have done. May your living word engrave my heart like a living stone, that I may leave a legacy of your love and grace to those I leave behind.

As Long as You
Have a Man

✠

For in him we live and move and have our being. . . .

ACTS 17:28

I WAS APPROACHING the end of a three-year relationship when my grandmother asked me the question yet again: "Are you still with your boyfriend, Kariña?"

I didn't bother with the mess of telling her I wasn't happy anymore . . . that the three years had distanced me from my relationship with God. I knew my boyfriend wasn't the man for my life, but she only wanted to hear one thing. "Yes," I said with a little smile.

"Oh, honey, I'm so happy," she replied, content to walk away and leave it at that. No further inquiry was necessary. I was a woman, I needed a man, and praise be to God I had one. End of story.

My grandmother lived in a world where becoming a wife was the first duty of womanhood—just before getting pregnant and hanging out in the kitchen all your life. The last few steps down the aisle to the altar on her wedding day brought a woman to her ultimate destination. Until then, she had been waiting around in the back of the church—and life itself—with nothing much to do. Although I had a desire to share my life with someone, I knew my worth and purpose didn't start after marriage.

After the breakup, I went to the altar in prayer. I'd forgotten my first love, the one who knew me better than I knew myself and who loved me without limits. I asked Him to redirect my life according to His will, not mine and vowed to listen to His voice as I lived out my purpose.

Throughout the years, God has been faithful, filling my life with love, laughter, family, and friends. He's allowed me to be used for His glory through my work and in various ministries in the church. I've also had the opportunity to travel and experience the world in beautiful and exciting ways.

If my grandmother were alive today, she'd be very concerned about her thirty-year-old single granddaughter, who has yet to give her life to a man. But I'm content to leave my life in God's capable hands—the hands that have held me up so far. If He has a husband and family to place in my future, that will be a wonderful new chapter in my life. Until then, however, you will not find me in the back of the church, waiting for life to begin. I'm already at the altar.

Prayer

Lord, help me not to focus on the schedule and pattern of others. I will rely on your timing and rest in the perfect plan you have for my life. Help me to learn and grow as you present each new experience in my life. Guide each step I take as I live, move, and have my being in you.

OH, WHAT BIG HIPS
YOU HAVE!

✛

But in fact God has arranged the parts in the body,
every one of them, just as he wanted them to be.
If they were all one part, where would the body be?

1 CORINTHIANS 12:18–19

I MAJORED IN fine arts in high school and took a variety of
classes, from sculpture to oil painting. One of these classes was
a course in fashion design, and, as with all my art classes, I plunged
into the projects with great interest and enthusiasm. I enjoyed de-
signing new styles of clothing for the models I drew. Each of my
models had big brown eyes and thick, curly brown hair. As a matter of fact, *thick* was a word you could use to describe most of them.
I gave my models a generous breast size and hips as wide and
round as those of most women I knew.

My teacher would walk around the class, tapping her pencil on
her tight lips, lingering over our shoulders as we drew. One time,
as she came to my desk, she practically shrieked. "Oh my God!

What's going on with those hips? What model has hips like those?"

I turned to look at her bewildered face. "Mine does," I responded—an answer she was unwilling to accept.

"Fix it," she said curtly as she walked away.

I looked over at the other students nearby. None of their models looked like mine. I got up to look at the drawings done by the rest of the class, but their models were all the same—tall, white, and superslim—a single definition for beauty. These women were apparently the only ones worthy of our design.

My models never turned into Barbie, but I slimmed them down enough to fit the standard and get through the class. Now I wish I'd made those hips even bigger, instead of squeezing into someone else's ideal; but that's what we all do to some degree. Someone has designed an idea of what beauty is, and we all do our best to fit within it. This narrowly defined image of beauty fits a ridiculously small percentage of women. It's an ingenious plan, because if the image fit the general population, there'd be nothing to sell to that vast majority seeking an unattainable ideal. There's so much money to be made, and keeping women in a constant state of insecurity and self-loathing seems to work. So while we're drinking powdered diet shakes and spending hours on the StairMaster, the "beauty" industries are bingeing on our dollars.

Here's a cheaper solution. Let's forget what the magazines, films, and television ads say about beauty. Let's reconstruct our ideas of beauty based on the influence of the greatest designer of all time, and discover the true meaning of beauty. His creations come in all shapes, colors, and styles—and everything He makes is beautiful in His eyes.

Prayer

Creator God, I thank you for making me the person I am. Help me to have a positive self-image, one that transcends what others think of me. Help me to treasure and take care of my body—your temple—by eating healthy food and exercising. I want my body to be what you intended when you created me—special, unique, and wonderfully made.

ISLAND OF COFFEE
AND MILK

☩

*As the deer pants for streams of water, so my soul pants for you,
O God. My soul thirsts for God, for the living God.
When can I go and meet with God?*

PSALM 42:1–2

I WATCHED IN HORROR as Doña Petra turned the television
on for my sister and me. My favorite cartoon was in Spanish!
What in the world was Popeye saying to Olive? Everything is in
Spanish! I screamed silently in my mind, as I forced a smile and
said thank you. She walked back to her kitchen, content to leave us
on the plastic-covered couch with blank stares on our faces.

My first trip to Puerto Rico was not the paradise I'd envisioned
it would be. Instead of lounging on sandy white beaches, we were
dragged from one house to another. The adults sat around drinking café con leche and talked in a language that was still gibberish
to me. During the day, our only source of entertainment was chas-
ing the chickens and roosters in the backyard. At five o'clock in the

morning, they'd get their revenge and chase us from peaceful dreams with their loud shrieks. The mosquitoes, apparent allies of poultry, would join the attack by buzzing in our ears and biting into our flesh, until we were covered with itchy red spots. When we finally boarded the plane back to New York City, I waved good riddance to this island of boredom and coffee.

In my late teens, I began to take a greater interest in my roots. The more stories I heard about life in Puerto Rico, the more I wanted to experience it for myself. I'd fallen in love with the music and language, yet I felt disconnected to my heritage. When my father decided to take a trip to Puerto Rico, I jumped at the chance to go. Once there, I absorbed all the sights and sounds around me. I was even happy to see the chickens and roosters. I no longer dragged my feet as we went from house to house to drink café con leche. I was now thirsty for the different stories people told of my father and grandparents. The trip connected me with my roots, and for the first time, I felt like a true Puerto Rican. When I boarded the plane for the second time to New York City, my heart ached.

When I think of these two very different experiences in Puerto Rico, it reminds me of my spiritual journey. As a child, I wasn't exactly a volunteer on Sunday mornings, waiting anxiously to go to church. I'd sit next to my mother, bored and restless, praying only that the service would end—now! Just like Spanish cartoons, the language of Christianity was gibberish to me. It wasn't until I was sixteen years old and had truly accepted Christ in my life that my relationship with God changed. My love for Him sparked a real desire to know Him better. I wanted to connect with Him and my identity as His child. I go to church now, no longer as a restless child. It's like sitting in a house in Puerto Rico, drinking café con leche and hearing stories that quench my soul.

Prayer

Lord, thank you for the living water of your word. May I be like the Samaritan woman by the well, eager to satisfy the thirst of my soul. May I be "a spring of water welling up to eternal life" (JOHN 4:14).

FACTORY

*"Come to me, all you who are weary and burdened, and I will give
you rest. Take my yoke upon you and learn from me, for I am gentle
and humble in heart, and you will find rest for your souls."*

MATTHEW 11:28–29

HEAVY ROLLS of wool leaned against the walls of the textile
factory, waiting to be measured and cut. Gloria watched the
men lift and carry them off, as if they were hospital stretchers with
patients covered in coarse blankets. Just a few months earlier, she
had been caring for patients who would enter the hospital in this
manner, but she was no longer in Honduras and no longer the nurse
she'd studied so hard to become. Instead of treating the sick, she was
tending to yards of unrolled fabric in New York City. The work was
tedious and unrewarding, but even factory work in America paid
more than nursing had in her impoverished little town.

There weren't many work options available to her in New York
City. Her papers were limited to a green card, and the language

barrier made it difficult to find a job that matched her abilities. In the factory, she'd measure and cut the thick material for hours, until her hands were sore. As time went on, her hands got used to the work, but there was so much she had to adjust to—the surprising cold, the noisy city life, and a new language. The hardest adjustment, however, was being away from her children. Her six-year-old son and four-year-old daughter had remained in Honduras with her mother.

Every week, when she received her pay from the factory, she remembered whom the sacrifice was for. When she'd go to the post office to send money to her children, it made her arms feel less empty. Years later, they were able to join her in America.

Our beautiful family friend has now retired from her labor after twenty-nine years of working in factories. Her children finished their education in America, and both enjoy professional careers. Thanks to their mother, who exchanged her skills and passion for her family's survival, they can live out their dreams and reach any goal they choose.

The sewing machines sound like an old rusty train,
one that screams in circles, going nowhere.
I press the pedal and push fabric through the quick, shiny needle.
It has tasted the blood of my finger more than once.

With the last seam stitched, I raise my head,
A luxury for my neck.
I see the women around me, who speak my language and
wear my face.
Their heads are down and their hands are busy on dresses
they'll never wear.

I hold the thin white dress in my coconut-colored hands,
and see beyond its birthplace of poor immigrant women,
fancy parties, romantic dinners, a walk-in closet.

Images fade as I reach into the basket of incomplete dresses,
jagged cut fabric.
The cry of my machine joins the others
as I press the pedal and lower my head once again.

Prayer

Lord, I put the raw fabric of my life into your care and trust the craftsmanship of your hands. Your word tells me, " 'For I know the plans I
have for you,' declares the LORD, 'plans to prosper you and not harm
you, plans to give you a hope and a future' " (JEREMIAH 29:11).

THE SPANISH MARKET

✤

". . . come, buy and eat! Come, buy wine and milk without
money and without cost. Why spend money on what is not bread,
and your labor on what does not satisfy? . . ."

A S I OPEN the bright red doors of *la marqueta*, I enter a world
of long ago, where my small fingers were nestled in my grandmother's hand. She would lead me through the crowd with a swift
grace, past the tall wooden stands that surrounded us. Boxes of
large red peppers, yellow and green bananas, onions, and coconuts
formed the belly of each booth. Large sacks of rice were piled up
near the counter, where bottles of olive oil sat waiting to be sold.
Tall stalks of sugarcane—the kind my father cut down as a youth
in Puerto Rico—leaned against the walls. The soda and juice con-
tainers had pictures of palm trees on them and came in such flavors as pineapple, coconut, guava, and mango.

Once Alela had examined the goods with her expert hands and

filled her basket with what she wanted, we'd walk back to her small apartment on Montrose Avenue. The fragrance of the market would rise again faintly as we emptied the bags in the sunlit kitchen. She'd pace back and forth between the sink and the stove, rinsing and cutting, as the air slowly filled with the aroma of her cooking.

As I stand here now, I watch and breathe in the memories. I walk past the stands of endless fruits and vegetables, through a crowd of strangers so familiar to me, in a world as delicious as my grandmother's cooking.

Prayer

Lord, you have provided me with a feast of blessings. Thank you for all the wonderful array of loved ones and special moments that fill my life. I've paid nothing to deserve such a reward. But like my salvation, which you've paid in full, I need only to accept these free gifts with a grateful heart.

Two Cooks

Do nothing out of selfish ambition or vain conceit, but in humility consider others better than yourselves. Each of you should look not only to your own interests, but also to the interests of others.

Philippians 2:3–4

As I step off the elevator, I can already smell the mouthwatering meal being prepared. I follow the aroma through the hallway and over to the door, inhaling with a smile as I take out my keys.

"Mi Kariña!" Papi says with a smile as I come in.

I walk over to the stove, where he's adjusting the flame. "Mmmm, Papi, that smells so good," I say as I take off my coat and give him a kiss. Papi cooking dinner is nothing new in our home. I grew up with that familiar image of him in the kitchen, adding spices and singing opera to an audience of onions and peppers. If he's not cooking, then my mother is, and most times it's both of them slicing, peeling, tasting, and stirring—working out their kitchen choreography together.

The image in many other Hispanic homes, however, looks significantly different. Most men don't even make it close enough to the stove to serve their own plate. They sit on their plastic-covered thrones and wait for their wives to set it before them and pour their juice.

When it was less common for women to work, taking responsibility for the home was a reasonable balance for a partnership of marriage. Yet today, when the majority of married couples in America hold full-time jobs, throwing the weight of all domestic duties on women is an unfair tilt of the scales.

It's even worse when Christian men defend this cultural machismo as a biblical principle. In J. Lee Grady's book *10 Lies the Church Tells Women* (Creation House, 2000), he points out ways the Bible has been misused to support such ideas, keeping women in a state of spiritual and emotional bondage. "It is a cultural bias, not a spiritual or scientific principle that women were made for the kitchen or laundry room . . . the important issue is that they listen to the Holy Spirit's guidance and seek His will for their situation."

Both my parents have held full-time jobs throughout their marriage. I've watched them share responsibilities in the home all my life. Whether it's laundry, dusting, or mopping the floor, they work together as true partners. As I see my mother and father working together in the kitchen even now, I can't help but smile at their perfectly wonderful recipe.

Prayer

Thank you, Father, for married couples who truly love and honor each other, and the example they give to others. Help me to respect and value others in all my relationships. Guide me with your Holy Spirit, that I may know how to fairly share responsibilities with those I love.

WHAT'S IN A NAME?

⚜

*". . . Bring my sons from afar and daughters from the ends of
the earth—everyone who is called by my name, whom I
created for my glory, whom I formed and made."*

ISAIAH 43:6–7

BECKY, MARY, LISA, KATE. My aunt looks pointlessly at the
large display of colorful coffee mugs, each one with a neatly
printed name across the front. She's drawn to those shelves in a
quest to find the impossible—her name. "Irma," she growls under
her breath, looking once again at the void between Irene and Jane.
"Why did they name me Irma?"

She's never liked her name, the way it snarls in its hostile English
pronunciation and its exclusion from the all-American souvenir
club. When her son was born, she gave him a name that would
blend. "Kevin," she says, smiling as she reaches for a coffee mug in
the *K* section.

My mother walks over to the display and finds her name in an instant—not her real birth name, which is Concepción, but the name she gave herself at the age of nine. She had been washing her hands in the school bathroom, when she looked and saw a large girl hovering over her. "I don't like your name," the girl said calmly before shoving my mother away from the sink. After the fight, she baptized herself with the name Connie. It's what everyone calls her to this day. She puts her mug in the basket, then adds two others, these with the names Karen and Diane. My name and my sister's can be found on any souvenir key chain or glass across America, written proof, perhaps, that we belong.

We've all grown up with the image of America displayed on television, in magazines, and behind endless store windows. While the advertisements don't often reflect a true image of America, most consumers are eager to buy in to it. Sold on this image, my aunt and mother make their way to the counter, content with the choices they've made. They take out their wallets as the cashier rings up another successful sale.

Prayer

Lord, your name is above all, and in your awesome love you have called me by that name. Help me to honor my identity in you, regardless of whether or not it blends into my environment.

COVERED

✛

He will cover you with his feathers, and under his wings you will find refuge; his faithfulness will be your shield and rampart. You will not fear the terror of night, nor the arrow that flies by day . . .

PSALM 91:4–5

DARKNESS ALWAYS terrified me as a child. At night, I would lie frozen on my back with my eyes squeezed shut, begging for unconsciousness. My bed was like a waiting room of torture, where sleep always took its time to come. Every inch of my body had to be covered; I feared exposing myself to the images of terror I imagined nearby. The cotton sheets served as a shield of protection, but they never eased my fears.

The only nights I felt completely safe were those I spent with my grandmother. I would pull the thick quilt up to my chin and nestle into her warm arms. In her pitch-black bedroom, my grandmother would begin to pray. Soft Spanish whispers filled the darkness with passion and a love for God. I didn't know what she was saying, but her words were a lullaby that caressed me into a deep sleep. I thought the warm quilt that covered me at my grandmother's had superpower, one hundred times more than my blankets at home.

Years have passed, and my night terror is gone. So is my grandmother. I miss those nights of being scooped in her arms underneath the quilt. I never thought I'd feel that warmth and protection again, until one day it revisited me.

The everyday terrors of life had been lurking nearby that morning as I walked to my church. My shield of protection felt as flimsy as a thin cotton sheet. I kissed some of my church family good morning and knelt near a chair as we began an intercessory prayer. One of my beautiful sisters in Christ began to pray for me. Her prayers filled the darkness I'd been feeling in my life, and in an instant, I felt the same peace I'd felt lying next to my praying grandmother. It was then that I understood the true source of that peace.

There was no power in that bed, in my grandmother's arms, or in her quilt. It was God's holy love spoken through my grandmother that eased my fear. The warmth of God's love can never be taken away—neither by death nor time—and it covers me like my grandmother's quilt.

Prayer

O God of Heaven, you are my light and my salvation; whom shall I fear? Help me realize that the night shines in the darkness and is the same as the light of day to you. I am not hidden from you. Thank you for the comfort of your all-encompassing love. Gather me under your protection like the hen gathers her chicks under her wings.

A Different Rhythm

He put a new song in my mouth, a hymn of praise to our God.
Many will see and fear and put their trust in the LORD.

PSALM 40:3

THE CARAVAN of three cars eased up toward the house trimmed with Christmas lights in the windows. We closed the car doors softly, trying hard to contain our laughter and excitement. Jackie rang the bell, and when the door finally opened, we exploded into song and clapping. We marched past Jackie's cousin, whose happy wide eyes were full of shock. She joined us as we paraded loudly through the living room, kitchen, and dining room. Other family members stopped what they were doing, putting down newspapers, forks, and remote controls, and joined us as we sang the lively Spanish Christmas songs. I danced around, clapping my hands, excited about my first *parranda*. This Puerto Rican version of Christmas caroling was something I'd only heard of but which I'd always wanted to experience.

I'd flown down to Miami to spend the last days of the holiday season with my friend's family. The whole week danced with the same energy and Hispanic rhythm as the *parranda*, yet in that atmosphere I suddenly felt oddly Caucasian. I was enthusiastic to take in all the flavors of that week, as if they were part of a foreign dish, exotic and new.

I hadn't realized how Americanized my family had become. The Hispanic rhythm we'd once possessed had slowly evolved into a different song, and I had never noticed. When I was younger, there was a quickness about my family that moved with a sweet chaos, and its rhythm was topped off with mostly Spanish voices. Everything centered around my grandparents, who brought the culture alive and set the pace for all of us. Their small apartment was always filled with people and energy, and the Hispanic neighborhood provided the faint background music of salsa in the street.

When we gather together now, the atmosphere has a different tone. Instead of taking place in the Hispanic neighborhood in Brooklyn, our family gatherings are held in the country, with its music of birds and swaying leaves. The once-cramped quarters are now more spacious, and the energy is more contained. We come together less often, with outdoor barbecues replacing weekly Sunday dinners of rice and beans, and the voice of our new song is English.

On the plane ride back to New York City, I had visions of all the changes I was going to initiate when I joined my family. We were going to get together more often and make an effort to speak in Spanish only! For Christmas, instead of singing "Silent Night," we were going to sing "Noche de Paz." I was going to buy some new salsa CDs and have my parents teach me to make *pasteles* and real Hispanic beans—from the bag, not the can. I could feel the rhythm coming back already. I was even planning our first *parranda*.

After a week or so, my enthusiasm faded, as I swayed once more to the rhythm of my surroundings. I also realized, however, that it wasn't completely void of Hispanic flavor. In a Puerto Rican family where most of the members were raised in America, the blending of two rhythms is inevitable. We're moving to what feels natural, and I can't force the hips to shake faster than the music is going. Yet as I dance to this mixture now, I pay especially close attention to the Hispanic side, making sure in my own way that its music never fades completely away.

Prayer

Lord, just as those who juggle their identity within two cultures, I find myself sometimes juggling my identity in you with the surroundings of this world. Please help me to never to lose the flavor of the Spirit, which you have placed in my heart.

STUFFED WITH LOVE

Offer hospitality to one another without grumbling. Each one should use whatever gifts he has received to serve others, faithfully administering God's grace in its various forms.

1 PETER 4:9–10

B LESSED IS ANY repairman who does work in my aunt Ali's house. There's no need for him to grab a sandwich at the deli when he's finished his job. She's going to sit him down at the table and give him a large plate of home-cooked food before he walks out of the door. Anyone who goes to her home is going to be fed— even if she's not expecting company. She has a habit of cooking extra just in case, so there's always more than enough.

Sitting at her table is like plunging into a new kind of extreme sport. You're always testing the limits of how much can fit in your stomach. Don't even think about serving yourself a flimsy plate. "That's it?" she'll gasp. "Take some more; there's plenty." The food is so amazing that you dread the point when you can't take another bite—and even then, you manage a few more. "Cake?" she chirps with a smile as you sit there unable to move, your belt loosened to the last hook.

My aunt has no problem expressing her love with kisses, hugs, and a warm smile. But to confirm to you how she feels, she has the perfect recipe. There are no frozen TV dinners or shortcuts in her kitchen; everything's made with loving patience and careful attention. No how-to books or measuring tools, either. "But how many teaspoons?" her daughters would ask, trying to learn that special touch. "You just know," she'd say, tasting, smelling, and stirring in more pepper.

When the plates are cleared from the table, you wobble over to the apartment terrace, where there's always a delicious breeze from the Hudson River. Feeling the maternal caress of that gentle wind, you close your eyes and rest in a warm cushioned chair, your stomach and your soul stuffed with love.

Prayer

Dear God, thank you for those who express their love in abundance. Help me to open my home and share my time and talents with love and sincerity. I pray that others might find comfort and the warmth of your Holy Spirit in me.

Papi's Hands

✠

Whatever you do, work at it with all your heart,
as working for the Lord, not for men, since you know that you
will receive an inheritance from the Lord as a reward.
It is the Lord Christ you are serving.

COLOSSIANS 3:23–24

I N PUERTO RICO, my father worked in sugarcane fields, cutting the sweet rods with a large machete. With each sugarcane harvest, he came closer to saving enough money to move to America, where eventually he traded his machete for dish-washing gloves. He washed away mashed potato and egg bits until he moved up to the job of short-order cook, making sandwiches and salads.

His many years of restaurant work ended when he married my mother and she found him a position at the company where she worked. He guarded trucks for an armored-truck company and took side jobs to earn extra money. When I was nine years old, he bought a large orange truck, where he sold hot dogs, cold drinks, and candy. I was in sugar heaven until he sold the truck and, for a short time, drove a taxi.

When my mother started working in a Brooklyn hospital, she again found him a position. He worked as a maintenance mechanic while he studied in seminary, and he repaired washing machines on the side. After graduation, he served as the pastor of a small Spanish-speaking church on the Lower East Side for fourteen years.

When I was growing up, I never gave much thought to how my father made a living. The hands that used to wash dishes were the same hands that washed jelly off my face. The hands that made sandwiches for strangers also prepared homemade soup when I was sick. I really don't know what customers thought of this man who took their lunch orders, but he was my father, my comedian, my teacher, and the joy of my heart.

He once apologized to my sister and me for not doing more to provide the financial stability he so wanted to give us. I'm not sure he'll ever truly understand how rich he's made my life and how proud I am of him. Whether wielding the machete in the sugarcane fields or holding forth the Sword of the Spirit from the pulpit, he's dedicated the labor of his hands to the Lord and to his family. I grew up resting my life in those capable hands, just as he rested his life, and ours, in the hands of his Father . . . his heavenly Father.

Prayer

Heavenly Father, give me the strength and the right attitude in all my labors. In everything I do, use me for your purpose and glory.

LATIN TEMPER

In your anger do not sin ...

EPHESIANS 4:26

M Y NON-HISPANIC FRIENDS love to watch me explain
something I'm passionate about. My facial expressions become exaggerated, my voice gets louder, and my arms flail about in
my own sign language. I can't help it. These elements spring to the
surface without any thought. I barely even realize what I'm doing
until someone points it out. "Wow, Karen, you're so animated,"
they comment. Yet most of the Hispanics I know are just as ex-
pressive when they speak.

In my experience, an explosive expressiveness is part of Hispanic
culture. Love is expressed vocally and then showers of kisses and
hugs confirm it. Since love, joy, and mere conversation are expressed with such vigor, anger usually follows the same rhythm.

Most passionate people find it difficult to balance how they feel with how enthusiastically they express it, especially in situations of anger. Sometimes, even when we're not that upset, the manner in which we explain our point of view can be perceived as aggressive. "What do you mean, 'Stop yelling'?" we'll shout. "I'm not yelling!"

There will be moments when we feel anger. While the Bible does not condemn this natural emotion (Ephesians 4:26), it does show us fruitful ways to express anger. Living a godly life is not an open invitation to receive abuse, and we are never called to ignore a negative situation. However, we must express our frustration in ways that will not dishonor God, ourselves, and others.

In upsetting situations, I have to remind myself to think before I speak and to pay especially close attention to my body language and voice volume so that my passion won't be misinterpreted as wrath. Above all, I must always ask God to guide my behavior and reactions in all circumstances, particularly the frustrating ones.

Prayer

Lord, help me to be an understanding listener and a gracious speaker. May my speech always be seasoned with discernment and used with restraint. I echo the words of the psalmist who said, "May the words of my mouth and the meditation of my heart be pleasing in your sight, O LORD, my Rock and my Redeemer" (PSALM 19:14).

RAISING KINGS

*From him the whole body, joined and held together
by every supporting ligament, grows and builds itself
up in love, as each part does its work.*

EPHESIANS 4:16

MY AUNT reluctantly left her Manhattan studio apartment to move back in with her parents in Brooklyn. Family and friends carried the heavy boxes of items she'd collected while living on her own. They didn't let her touch a thing; the single mother-to-be was already carrying enough weight of her own.

Throughout her pregnancy, she did her best to readjust to the strict rules in the traditional home she'd happily left two years before. Her parents' disapproval made it even harder, but whatever anger they carried gave birth to joy when they finally held their grandson in their arms. Ah, yes, a king was born, and they couldn't have been any happier to serve him—especially my grandmother.

Thus began the battle of two mothers, each one with her own firm ideas about raising my cousin.

When he was an infant, they fought over how he should be fed. My grandmother couldn't tolerate those flimsy, modern diets suggested by those *sangano* doctors. "I didn't raise you kids like that!" she'd bark. "You're starving him!"

The struggle only intensified as he grew older. My cousin was the little macho of the house and my grandmother waited on him hand and foot. When he was old enough for chores, my grandmother asked him only to take out the garbage and run to the *bodega* to pick up bread. These were acceptable tasks designed for a man. If my aunt asked him to sweep or wash the dishes, the broom or sponge would be snatched from his hands. "You're going to let your son do a woman's work?" my grandmother would shout. "Are you raising him to be a housewife?" My cousin was no fool, and he quickly learned to hide behind my grandmother's ideas when it suited him. Outnumbered and fed up, my aunt would usually give in after an argument.

My cousin's two umbilical cords were cut when he moved upstate to attend a university there. Now he had no choice but to cook his own meals, wash his own dishes, and sweep his own floors. He continued to do for himself after he graduated and moved out on his own. He kept an immaculate house, especially the kitchen, which he considered sacred—just as my grandmother did.

When he got married, however, the little king my grandmother had created did his best to put the crown back on his head. As the man of the house, there were certain chores he felt he didn't have to do anymore. His wife, on the other hand, had grown up struggling with those same gender-role issues in her own Hispanic family. There was no way she was going to let it continue in her married life. The couple's heated debates reflected the arguments of my aunt and grandmother, but this time, stubborn tradition would not prevail. While my aunt was usually the one to give in, my cousin admits that now he's the one who'll cook a dinner or sweep the floors to keep the peace.

As for my aunt in all this, she's found a new role to play—that of grandmother. "Why are you still feeding the baby that powdered water after six months?" she complains. "You're starving him!"

Prayer

Lord, even though we're all raised in ways that reflect cultural mind-sets and traditions, please direct my actions according to your will. "Show me your ways, O LORD, teach me your paths; guide me in your truth and teach me, for you are God my Savior, and my hope is in you all day long" (PSALM 25:4–5).

LOSING MY MIND

☩

Do not be anxious about anything, but in everything, by prayer and petition, with thanksgiving, present your requests to God. And the peace of God, which transcends all understanding, will guard your hearts and your minds in Christ Jesus.

PHILIPPIANS 4:6–7

THE MOMENT I walked into the cabin with my heavy bags, the faint smell of urine made me want to go back on the bus to New York City. The money was good, and the thought of working with mentally challenged kids seemed interesting, but now I stood in a room heavily stocked with diapers of all sizes and latex hospital gloves.

The other counselors were already fixing up the prisonlike beds, so I put down my things and headed for a large bag of white sheets. I walked around a little girl no older than seven who was making cute little noises on the floor. My stomach turned as I passed the huge fifteen-year-old with the obvious bulge in her pants. There's no way I'm touching that diaper, I thought, reaching for a pillowcase.

When the beds were all fixed, we headed to the dining hall for a late breakfast. My empty stomach groaned with hunger as we settled the girls into their seats. But before I could reach for a bagel, I found out that some of them needed to be hand-fed. Christina, the fifteen-year-old in diapers, needed her food to be mixed in the blender. I served her a plate of bagel bits, applesauce, and scrambled eggs blended into the perfect texture and color of vomit. After the sloppy feeding, my appetite was gone.

I spent the next hour at arts and crafts, scooping wet crayon bits out of mouths, cleaning paint off the floor, and smelling the odor of heavy diapers begging to be changed. When we got to the cabin, I raced for the youngest child and grabbed a bag of diapers marked SMALL. "I've got Kimberly," I yelled with a smile, relieved that someone else would have to change the older girls. The whole day passed at the same hectic speed, without a moment of rest. When we finally dressed the girls in pajamas and shut off the lights, I collapsed on the narrow bed, my nerves shot and my stomach empty.

The next morning, I had to drag myself out of bed. Five more days to go, I thought, putting on the latex gloves. The early risers had changed diapers and dressed all the kids except for Christina, who was still under the covers. I stood there for a second and then slowly walked over to the bag of extra-large diapers. She was lying on her bed, smiling and giggling to herself. Look at her, I thought. She has no idea. I tried to smile also and change my bad attitude as I pulled off her nightshirt. Maribelle, one of the other counselors, came over to help me, and changing her wasn't as awkward as I'd thought it would be. I realized that despite her size, Christine was as dependent on me as an infant.

Once she was dressed, I brushed Christina's hair and pulled it back into a neat ponytail, keeping it away from her light brown eyes. For a moment, she looked like any "normal" teenager. "Look how pretty you are," I said, trying to get her to look at me. But she just draped the sheet over her head and grabbed a plastic toy to bang on her ear.

By lunchtime, Christina was transformed into the image I had encountered the first day. Her hair was matted and her clothes were freshly stained from the morning's activities. My clothes were stained as well, and the nonstop work swallowed me back into exhaustion. I can't do this anymore, I thought, looking at the mashed potatoes smeared in Ana's hair. I reached for a napkin, wanting to cry. I cleaned her head, laughing to myself in frustration, feeling like I was going to snap any second and smear mashed potatoes all over my own hair. Just then, I heard a squeal of laughter from behind. I turned, to see Christina laughing uncontrollably and spraying milk out of her mouth. Milk was everywhere—on her face, on her clothes, and on Maribelle, the counselor who had been feeding her. Maribelle and I looked at each other in shock for about two seconds and then burst into laughter as loud as Christina's.

Upon my arrival, I had felt sorry for Christina and the others because of their inability to be part of the "real" world. But in that moment, I now understood and appreciated their world. Work and mess were driving me over the edge, while Christina sat right in the middle of it all, squealing with delight. She didn't care about the milk on the floor. And as I laughed, I didn't care, either.

Prayer

Help me to face new and challenging situations with the peace only you can give. I ask for your special care and blessing for those who face the daily struggle of mental and physical challenges. They live in a world that is centered around people without disabilities, and they are often more disabled by the obstacles we put in front of them. Thank you for their courage and ability to survive despite the difficulties. Teach me to face each day with the same strength.

IN MY OLD SAN JUAN

Though I scatter them among the peoples,
yet in distant lands they will remember me. . . .

Zechariah 10:9

W HEN MY FATHER was a child in Puerto Rico, he would often visit an older family friend who lived nearby. My father was always drawn to the guitar hanging silently on the wall, and when the old man noticed the interest, he took it down for the curious little boy. His aged fingers danced over the strings and he began to sing the beautiful folk songs of Puerto Rico. This sparked in my father such a desire to learn that he soon became the old man's pupil.

Music had always brought my father pleasure, but when he moved to New York as a young man, it took on a deeper meaning. New York was an alien world of English and concrete. Tropical days and warm nights were replaced with frosty wind and shocking snow.

There were no landscapes of mountains, beaches, palm trees, and farmland. Here there were no horizons, and the endless buildings, which blocked the sky, were like bars. Inside, locked in small apartments, my father would play his guitar and sing of the island so far away. As he closed his eyes to sing, the small room would have no choice but to stretch its walls and make room for sugarcane fields, rain forests, fiery sunsets, and country roads.

All my life, my father has filled our home with these bittersweet songs of longing and joy. The one I've come to love the most is "En Mi Viejo San Juan." It's the one he sings with extra passion and the one that fully describes what he feels when singing. The songwriter speaks of the island he left behind to move to a land of strangers; but his heart, he says, he left by the oceanside in his old San Juan. He speaks of returning home one day. Toward the end of the song, the writer reveals he's too old and fragile to go back. He realizes he's going to die far from the island he loves so much.

Unlike the man in the song, my father has been able to revisit the island he left behind. Despite the difficulties and adjustments, he's found happiness in his new land, in the city. It's where he found his love, raised a family, and pastored a church. But during those times when the walls start closing in and the country boy wants to swim in rivers, climb trees, and run free in the open air, he closes his eyes and returns to Puerto Rico with his voice and a guitar.

Prayer

Lord, sometimes I feel distant from you, as if I were in another land. Help me to remember you and reach out to your Spirit with songs of praise.

SPANISH CORITOS

*Praise the LORD. Praise the LORD, O my soul. I will praise the
LORD all my life; I will sing praise to my God as long as I live.*

PSALM 146:1–2

WHEN I LEFT the Hispanic congregation I grew up with to
go to the English-speaking church to which I felt called, I
felt like a stranger in someone else's home. Although I was excited
to start a new journey in a place filled with so many possibilities, I
was sometimes homesick for the comfort and intimacy of my old
church. Things that had always felt natural and normal were gone.
I missed the beautiful old women who would hold my face in their
delicate hands, expressing words of love and blessings. I missed the
poetry of Spanish prayers and, perhaps more than anything else, I
missed the spiciness of our worship. Spanish congregations sing
coritos that are filled with energy and life. They make you want to

get out of your seat, clap your hands, and move your hips from side to side.

Coritos aren't just for Sunday mornings, either. Hispanic churches are so saturated with these songs that they're almost part of the language. During one of our congregation's frequent meals together, someone would start humming a *corito* while serving rice; someone else pouring soda would sing along, until eventually everyone in the room would be singing, moving, and creating instruments with cups and utensils. The music expressed our joy, our love for Christ, and the flavor of our wonderful culture.

Years later, I no longer feel like a stranger in my English-speaking church. Regardless of the differences in culture and worship, I feel like a real member of the family, and I know that God has placed me there for a purpose. The congregation has not only embraced me as one of their own, but they've embraced my Hispanic culture, as well. They've enthusiastically learned some Spanish *coritos* and have incorporated them in worship and praise. As I stand in the front to lead the songs, I watch the people get out of their seats, clap their hands, and sway their hips from side to side, singing with a flavor I know so well.

Prayer

Receive my thanksgiving through praise, O God! Thank you for putting a new song in my heart. I lift up my voice to you from the very depths of my being. May my songs of praise reach your ears as prayers of thanksgiving.

JOURNEY TO JEANS

... The LORD does not look at the things man looks at.
Man looks at the outward appearance,
but the LORD looks at the heart.

1 Samuel 16:7

WHY ARE YOU doing that?" I asked my mother as we got out of the car. She was rolling up her pants until they were hidden beneath her knee-length coat.

"Your grandfather," she replied, taking my hand to cross the street. We climbed the stairs and knocked on my grandparents' apartment door. "Mami," my mother said in an urgent whisper when my grandmother appeared, *"páseme una falda."* A few seconds later, my grandmother came back with a skirt for my mother to slip over her pants in the hallway. My mother had been wearing pants for as long as I could remember, but I'd never realized until then that she kept this a secret from my grandfather.

In my grandfather's time, respectful women in Puerto Rico never wore pants. Although he raised his kids in America, this belief was already set in his mind. This cultural idea had also found its way into most Hispanic churches in America, which only intensified his conviction. As an obedient daughter, my mother complied, never owning a pair of pants until she was a married woman.

The day my mother bought her first pair of jeans, she stared reluctantly at the pile of folded denim. Her determined sister rummaged through the pairs of jeans and found my mother's size. "Maybe I shouldn't do this yet," my mother mumbled. "It doesn't feel right." Her sister tossed a pair of jeans at my mother. "For crying out loud, Connie, just try them on!" Although she'd always wanted to wear pants, she wasn't sure if she was being disobedient to God or to a man-made regulation. She'd been raised with the prohibition about wearing pants, but there she was in the fitting room, trying them on for size.

My mother wore her new jeans a week later to an office picnic at Lake Welch. She got out of the car, cringing at her daring debut, and walked toward the crowd of coworkers, feeling naked. "That day was so strange," she recalled later. "Wearing pants felt so wonderful, but it was awkward, too. I felt liberated and guilty at the same time."

After that first pair, she added a few more to her wardrobe, yet she never wore them to church or during visits to her father, who was now bedridden. When she did wear them, she'd look over her shoulder, paranoid that she'd bump into one of the *hermanas* or *hermanos* from church. Little by little, however, her attitude changed.

Today, she has more pants in her closet than skirts and dresses combined, not to mention the shorts and open-toed shoes, attire that she would have never considered in the past. Her wardrobe now consists of a variety of styles, patterns, and colors—no longer in compliance with one mind-set or design. She has learned to let go of other people's convictions and live according to the ones God Himself has placed in her heart.

Prayer

Lord, thank you for looking into my heart and knowing who I really am. Please remove any tendencies I may have to judge people based on their outward appearance. Help me to seek your will and to follow the Spirit's lead. When I find it too difficult, teach me to differentiate between what you really ask of your followers and what are purely cultural interpretations of Scripture.

ALL of HIS CHILDREN

✛

You intended to harm me, but God intended it for good to
accomplish what is now being done, the saving of many lives.

GENESIS 50:20

THE GREEN AND RED Christmas lights shimmered off the
shreds of wrapping paper that lay scattered on the floor. The
kids were jumping around the small apartment, excited about their
gifts. It was the first time their father could afford to splurge on
good presents, and he was enjoying the reaction of his son and
daughter.

That Christmas took place before I was born—before my parents fell in love. My father was celebrating the holidays with his
family, the only one he thought he'd ever know. He couldn't imagine life without them, especially during such happy moments as
those. But just a few weeks later, his wife announced she was leaving him and sending the children to Puerto Rico. My brother and

sister were sent to be raised by their aunt and grandmother, while their mother remained in New York with another man. My father mourned the loss of his family in the empty and silent apartment.

Years later, my father was celebrating another Christmas—this one with my mother, my sister, and me. As we opened the gifts he bought us, it must have been bittersweet to watch us jump around the apartment as his kids had done years before. Although we enjoyed visits with my brother and sister, the time was always too short and the good-byes were always tearful.

When we reunite as a family to celebrate the holidays now, the tears of the past have lost their sting. The excitement of being together keeps us up late into the night as we cuddle up with one another, laughing and talking for hours. My favorite moments are when my brother takes out a guitar and we sing old Puerto Rican folk songs like "Lamentos Borincano" and "En Mi Viejo San Juan." All of us sing, harmonizing in different chords. My father closes his eyes as he belts out his tenor part, enjoying these sweet moments with all his children.

Prayer

Thank you, Lord, for turning painful situations into joyous ones. Help me during those times when I can't see beyond the sadness of my situation. Remind me that you have the power to turn tears of sadness into tears of joy.

MARTHA, MARTHA

Unless the LORD builds the house,
its builders labor in vain. . . .

PSALM 127:1

T HERE'S NOT ENOUGH food!" This is what I was told two hours before the church anniversary dinner. All the guests, including the ones we weren't expecting, were sitting comfortably in the air-conditioned sanctuary. I ran out in the summer haze in my new high heels and raced to get the ingredients for our stand-in chef. I carried back two heavy bags and emptied them on the table. "Okay," he said, already sweating from the heat of the kitchen, "wash those and then chop that." After completing my tasks, I ran into the dining area to see how things were going. The lights were off and the tables weren't set up yet! I ran upstairs to the sanctuary to find someone to help me. Ah, the air conditioning felt great, but two minutes later I was back in the hot kitchen, pulling out enormous folding tables with the help of a friend.

"Karen," the chef cried out, "I'm going to need some more peppers and another package of ground meat." Off I went again, running in heels that were now cutting into my skin. For two hours, I didn't stop. At one point, I had to run upstairs, catch my breath, wipe the sweat off my face, and sing a solo for the service that was taking place. It was the only moment of peace before going back to work downstairs.

I wasn't responsible for planning this event, but for some reason most of its last-minute mess fell on me. I was exhausted. Finally, the guests came down to the dining area, and I stood behind the food tables, filling plates. My stomach was growling, my nerves were shot, and my feet were destroyed.

This day was especially intense, but juggling multiple tasks was nothing new. When you attend a small church, you have to make up for the lack of hands—especially when you're the pastor's daughter. I had so many responsibilities that when I thought of church, the image that came to mind was work. Communion with God came second. Even if I tried to push it to the side, the workload seemed to cry out for my attention.

When I got home that evening, I was completely drained. I thought about my friend's church, the one I had been visiting on and off for a year. Each time I left their worship services, I felt fed, refreshed, and in touch with God. I couldn't remember the last time I had felt that way after returning home from mine. Lord, I prayed, I don't know what to do. Part of me wishes I could just go to this other church, but how can I leave my church when there's just so much to do? Who is going to do everything?

That night, I was reading the Gospel of Luke. I had been reading a chapter each night and was up to chapter ten. When I reached verse thirty-eight, God answered my prayer as clearly as if He were sitting right next to me. It read:

As Jesus and his disciples were on their way, he came to a village where a woman named Martha opened her home to him. She had a sister named Mary, who sat at the Lord's feet listening to what he said. But Martha was distracted by all the preparations that had to be made. She came to him and asked, "Lord, don't you care that my sister has left me to do the work by myself? Tell her to help me!"

"Martha, Martha," the Lord answered, "you are worried and upset about many things, but only one is needed. Mary has chosen what is better, and it will not be taken away from her."

With each word, the burden was lifted from my shoulders. I had been acting like a slave to a distant master, when all He really wanted was His daughter to sit at His feet and know Him as a Father and a friend.

Within the year, I became a member of my friend's church and dedicated my time there to strengthen my relationship with the Lord. I now serve in various ministries, but my service is no longer a priority. As for my old church, it hasn't fallen apart in my absence, as I so arrogantly feared. His church and its people rest in His hands, not mine.

Prayer

Dear God, thank you for communicating with me through your living Word. I know that "All Scripture is Godbreathed and is useful for teaching, rebuking, correcting and training in righteousness" (2 TIMOTHY 3:16). Help me meditate on your Word and communicate with you in daily devotion and prayer. Let me never put anything above my time with you.

FATHER FIGURE

✛

I will proclaim the decree of the LORD: He said to me,
"You are my Son; today I have become your Father."

M OST DAYS AFTER SCHOOL, my cousin sat with our grandfather at the corner pizzeria. Kevin's school-uniform tie
would rest carelessly next to the oregano and pepper as he'd stretch
the mozzarella from his lips in a long white string. "Papi," Kevin
would mumble, his mouth full of cheese and tomato sauce, "did
you bring the baseball?" Every day, after grabbing a bite to eat, the
two would make their way to the park for a few hours of catch. My
grandfather would fit his aged hands into the leather catcher's mitt
and hold it out for Kevin's fastballs. When the sky turned a deep
blue, they'd walk home together to the small apartment where they
lived with my aunt and grandmother.

Like many kids in the neighborhood, Kevin never knew his biological father. A one-parent home was a normal family structure where Kevin grew up, yet he had so much more. He called our grandfather "Papi" because that's the part he chose to take on.

Kevin's other father figure was his mother, who had to play the role of both parents, especially when it came to discipline. My grandfather, who was such an expert at laying down the law for his own kids, seemed to lose all such ability when it came to his grandson. If those two weren't enough to fill the void of his absent father, Kevin had a third father figure—his *tio*. My father and Kevin would run errands together, go fishing, and when Kevin pitched in Little League baseball games, his *tio* was in the stands with the rest of the family, rooting him on.

During one of those games, Kevin pitched a no-hitter. It was a proud moment, especially for him and our grandfather. The whole team signed the ball, which my cousin kept for many years after the game. When my grandfather died after a long illness, Kevin wrote his good-byes on an empty space on the old Little League ball and placed it in our grandfather's casket.

Years later, Kevin taught his own son how to pitch a ball, displaying the same love and patience he'd received so many years ago. As Kevin and his four-year-old sat together eating at the local pizzeria, his son, with a mouth full of sauce, asked him a question. "Daddy, where's your father?" Kevin was taken a bit by surprise, but after a moment, he simply answered, "I don't know; I've never met him."

Perhaps there's not a lot Kevin can say about a father whom he never knew. Yet he can always share the stories and pass on the love of those who happily filled his father's place.

Prayer

Dear heavenly Father, thank you for always providing for us according to each need. I lift up in prayer those who don't know their biological parents and ask that you continue to fill their lives with love, despite the absence. Above all, I thank you for receiving me as your child. You are a loving Father who will never leave my side.

At the Age of Ten

✣

I have been crucified with Christ and I no longer live, but Christ lives in me. The life I live in the body, I live by faith in the Son of God, who loved me and gave himself for me.

GALATIANS 2:20

MOTHER AND DAUGHTER were on their way to the movie theater when they approached the small church on the corner. The minister was standing outside when he saw the young woman with her daughter. It had been years since they'd last spoken, and when he called out the young woman's name, she hurried over to greet her old friend. My mother, who was ten years old at the time, quietly listened to the conversation. This friendly and relaxed discussion between the minister and her mother was something curious and new. All the church leaders she'd known before had seemed distant and unapproachable. They'd stand at the altar like frozen saints who were to be revered, not spoken to like friends.

Until then, everything my mother knew about God was like a box of loose puzzle pieces. The picture was unclear and she didn't even know how to start putting it together. There was a vague place called heaven and a scary place called hell, but how to get to the right one was a mystery. She was so fearful of going to hell, she used to pray that God would let her die as a child. All children go to heaven, she thought. If I die before I turn eleven, God has to let me live with him.

The minister invited them in for the evening service, which was about to start. There was something warm about the atmosphere, and that seemed unfamiliar in a church setting. It felt comfortable, like home. People who were strangers greeted her and her mother like close family friends. Mother and daughter were no longer going to see a film, as originally planned, but as she sat down before the service began, it was more exciting than any movie she'd ever seen.

Soon she was going to church every Sunday and on Wednesdays after school. The questions she had were beginning to be answered, and she no longer prayed for God to take her to heaven at the age of ten.

During one Wednesday service, the minister asked if anyone wanted to accept Christ into his or her life. My mother went to the front and dedicated her life to the Lord. When she gives her testimony now, she always says, "In a way, I did die at the age of ten, just as I had prayed. I died to myself so that Christ could live in me."

Prayer

Lord, even as adults, our image of you isn't always clear. Help me to continually seek clarity and revelations through your word. Thank you for those servants who teach and challenge others to know you better.

RENAISSANCE

✣

And if the Spirit of him who raised Jesus from the dead is living in you, he who raised Christ from the dead will also give life to your mortal bodies through his Spirit, who lives in you.

ROMANS 8:11

IT WAS ONE of those gloomy and depressing days. There was so much to do, but I had no motivation to move. Opting to wallow in my so-called misery, I attached myself to the comfort of my bed. The pillows were fluffed, the quilts were fresh and warm, and I'd just opened a large box of chocolate-chip cookies. I picked up the remote control and surfed through the channels, looking for something to watch.

I came across an interesting documentary about a group of elderly musicians in Cuba. After years of retirement, they had been given an opportunity to perform once again. Before one of their shows, the old men were shown lounging on chairs and beds in their hotel room. They looked as lifeless as I felt at that very moment. Their movements were slow and fragile-looking, as if life had begun to slip away. The next shot, however, took me by surprise. They were on the stage standing in front of an electrified audience. The guitarist, who had seemed to be on his deathbed seconds ago, was now dancing across the floor as he played his guitar. Another skeletal old man was sitting at the piano, his long fingers attacking the keys like frantic spiders. The energy they had as they created their wonderful music made me feel a little silly about lying on my bed in the middle of the afternoon.

How often we walk around like zombies in one way or another, as if there's no life left inside. We drag our feet through life, allowing disappointments, sadness, and stress to weigh us down. As I lay there watching the old men dancing on the stage, I decided that instead of burying myself in my mood, I would ask God to revitalize my spirit. I shook off the covers and danced to the rhythm of their music as I got ready to face the rest of the day.

The guitar lies voiceless and still,
near the sleeping old man.
The once-shiny varnish is faded and dull,
its color no longer a rich deep brown.

The old man wakes in the silence,
wrestling away from the deep call of sleep,
stretching his bones like a rusty music box.

He sits on the edge of his bed,
eyelids ticking like a silent clock,
then reaches to waken the sleeping guitar.

His cold fingers touch the still strings,
frozen veins brought back to life.
Music breathes from their mutual touch,
and emerges from silence like an infant born.

Prayer

Lord, I look to you in times of discouragement and weariness. You
have given me my life and your Spirit lives in me. Breathe new life into
me when I'm feeling empty and revive me with a sense of purpose in
your will.

PRESSING TOWARD
THE GOAL

*I press on toward the goal to win the prize for which
God has called me heavenward in Christ Jesus.*

PHILIPPIANS 3:14

O KAY, KAREN, you grab the yellow bag; I've got this one.
Connie, don't forget the sodas." My aunt Irma surveys the
situation, checking off the mental list of things to do. As usual, she
takes charge, showing us what to lift and where to put it. "Okay,
Gene, we're gonna need some help over here lifting this. Ready?
On my count—one, two, three."

The car is almost packed for another weekend getaway my aunt
has cooked up. She's definitely a leader, and most of the time, our
family needs one. Without her, growing up would have been a lot
less eventful. She was the one who'd get us out of the house and in-
volved in activities. Fairs, concerts, picnics, and vacations were all
made possible by our own event planner. She took me to my first

musical on Broadway when I was ten, introduced me to many different kinds of food, and constantly challenged me to do things I didn't think I could do—including my first roller-coaster ride. Irma was the fun aunt, the one I always wanted to be around, but more important, she was my second mother. My sister and I were the daughters she never had and the sisters to her only son.

On one of our outings, Irma doubled over in pain. She had been sick for quite a while with what they believed at the time was lupus. This, however, was the first time I had seen her in so much pain.

"Let's go, Aunt Irma," I said, nervous knots twisting in my stomach. "Let's just go home."

She squinted her eyes and looked at me as if she were trying to understand my words. "Are you kidding me?" she finally asked. "Honey, if I went home every time I felt pain, I'd never leave the house." After a few minutes of rest, she was back on her feet, our plans still intact.

I'd always known my aunt as a strong-willed person, but that moment was when I realized how strong she truly was. I admired, and continue to admire, her stubborn love of life. Years later, doctors rediagnosed her ailment as scleroderma. There are two types, and, thankfully, she has the tamer form.

"It's not the systemic type, which kills you," she says. "I have the one that just tortures you for the rest of your life." She doesn't let it stop her from doing what she wants and needs to do. She swallows her assortment of pills in the morning and takes off for work, a movie, or a great sale at Wal-Mart.

Now I throw the yellow bag in the car and we're finally ready to go. She gives everything a last survey and gets into the driver's seat.

"All right, are we ready?" she asks as she puts the key in the ignition. The engine starts and she pulls out of the garage with a smile. "And we're off!"

Prayer

Thank you, Lord, for the example of those who push forward in life without fear, despite their circumstances. Help me to learn from them, and give me the strength to live life with the same fierce determination.

FEAR OF FRYING

When I was a child, I talked like a child, I thought like a child,
I reasoned like a child. When I became a man,
I put childish ways behind me.

1 CORINTHIANS 13:11

I T NEVER MATTERED how soft the pillow felt, or how sleepy I was in the mornings. I was always quick to jump up and get ready for school. All my mother had to do was yell, "I'm going to get fired!" and I would rush around in a sick panic to get ready. Until I was about eight years old, I thought the word *fired* literally meant that her boss was going to burn her with fire if she was late for work.

We were always rushing in the morning, racing around barefoot, our hair unbrushed, as we looked for shoes, books, and swallowed our breakfast.

During school holidays or mornings when I woke up feeling sick, my mother would drive me to my grandmother's apartment.

She'd screech to a halt, beep the horn, then scramble with me to the front door. When my grandmother appeared above the long staircase in the hallway, my mother would yell, "Thanks, Ma," peck me on the forehead, and race back to the car. I'd take a deep breath, which was more like a sigh of relief, then walk nice and slowly up the stairs, toward the smell of bacon and eggs. My grandmother would slowly fill my plate while I sat at the table, adjusting to the sense of calm.

Those days I spent with her included walks to the store, where she'd buy all the necessities for her famous meals. On one particular day, we walked to one of our usual stops, a place I called "the chicken house." It was a large redbrick building, and you could always hear and smell it before reaching the entrance. Inside the large space were huge metal cages, one on top of the other. Each cage was packed tightly with noisy chickens struggling to reach the front, where their food was placed. I watched hundreds of heads poke through metal bars, pecking at the long yellow buckets of seed attached to their cages. A few chickens always walked freely on the floor, and I'd chase them to see how fast they could run.

That day, the man in the store greeted my grandmother as usual, exchanging words in Spanish as she pointed to one of the chickens behind the bars. I was already used to seeing him open a cage and grab a pair of skinny red legs. He'd walk with the chicken hanging upside down, the bird flapping its wings and leaving a trail of white feathers on the floor. As soon as the chicken was tied and weighed, he'd take it to a room toward the back and close the door.

This particular day, there were more people than usual in the store. My grandmother spoke to one of her neighbors while the man did his job faster than ever. One of the loose chickens was clucking slowly nearby. I lunged at her and she jumped with a squawk, sending a cloud of feathers in the air. I chased her around the store until I lost my breath. As I stopped to rest, I found myself standing near the mysterious back door, which had been left open by the busy worker. When I looked up, the man was holding an enormous knife over a screaming chicken. He quickly hammered the blade on its neck. I completely froze as he lifted the headless chicken and rushed out without noticing me.

After the beheading, I had a recurring nightmare, one that lasted for months. I was locked in a cage with my mother and grandmother, eating seeds from a yellow bucket, when I saw a giant chicken dressed as a little girl. Standing next to her was an even bigger grandma chicken, who was pointing at our cage. The three of us hugged and cried as this giant wing reached in and grabbed hold of my mother's red high heels.

When we had finished the shopping that afternoon, we went back to the apartment, where Alela prepared dinner. I listened to the chicken bubbling over the fire and cringed. When my plate was served, I sat at the table and ate every grain of rice and all my vegetables, including the broccoli, which I hated. I didn't touch the chicken.

"Eat your chicken," my grandmother said as she answered the telephone. I poked it with my fingers and even tore a piece off, but I didn't eat a bite. She came back and sat down at the table next to me. "That was your Mami. She's going to pick you up late, okay?"

"Why?"

"Because her boss wants her to work late."

"But why?"

"Because if she doesn't, he'll fire her." I froze in my chair. "And if your Mami gets fired, she can't buy you clothes and food anymore. You see what has to happen just so you can eat?"

I looked down at the cold, dead chicken lying on my plate and nodded a silent yes.

Prayer

Dear God, children are so new to this world. They often face situations without a clear understanding of truth. Their imaginations take off, creating fears and concerns that don't need to be. Lord, I am like a child. There are many things I don't understand about you and this world you've created. Let me grow into the answers by reading your Word. Lord, make me mature and give me understanding. I'm aware that not all my questions will be answered, but help me not to fear. I trust in your guidance, because you know all things.

PLUMP AND HEALTHY

*Dear friends, I pray that you may enjoy good health and that all
may go well with you, even as your soul is getting along well.*

3 JOHN 1:2

"¡QUE NIÑA SALUDABLE!" The women squeal with glee as
they take the baby from my cousin's arms. Her seven-
month-old little girl is the kind of baby with *muslos* you just want
to bite. Delighted, they squeeze her chubby little cheeks, arms, and
thighs, like kids opening a fresh batch of Play-Doh. "Ay, what a
healthy little girl!" they repeat, as if congratulating the mother on a
job well done.

For Hispanics, a little meat on the bones equals good health,
and it's always met with praise. "You've gained some weight!" is not
an open invitation to the StairMaster; it's a compliment. While a
slender, meatless figure is the American ideal, Hispanics, especially
the older generations, usually regard it with a sense of pity. The

same women who fuss over my cousin's healthy baby look at her thin six-year-old (who has a finicky appetite) and sigh, saying, "*Bendito*." They want nothing more than to take home a *pobre flaco* and perform an emergency transfusion of rice and beans.

However, the younger generations of Hispanics in America don't always share the same concept of body image. While the family is filling your plate for the second time and urging you to eat, the media is telling you to join the gym and get rid of that "embarrassing" weight. "Ever dream of having the perfect body?" they ask as a size-two model twirls in front of the camera. "Well, now you can, for only two hundred dollars a month." With the conflicting messages at home and on TV, movie screens, and in fashion magazines, Hispanic girls are trying to figure out what the true "perfect" figure is.

Catherine Shisslak, a professor at the University of Arizona College of Medicine, states, "A growing body of research indicates that minority females exhibit many of the same abnormal eating behaviors as white females." In the past, Hispanics were thought to be less affected by anorexia nervosa and bulimia, yet recent studies have challenged this misconception. In a society obsessed with thinness, it seems to be a growing challenge for girls to accept a different standard, regardless of their cultural influences.

For now, chubby Hispanic babies will continue to be praised for their plump cheeks and squeezable arms. In the future, however, when those compliments are overpowered by criticism, we can only wonder what kind of image they'll choose to embrace and how far they'll go to obtain it.

Prayer

Lord, despite the various perceptions of beauty within different cultures, help me honor my health over image, regardless of how my views are shaped. Thank you for the body you have given me. I pray for your guidance in the care of my body.

VIOLET KISSES

Taste and see that the LORD is good;
blessed is the man who takes refuge in him.

PSALM 34:8

T HE CLOCK was torturing me with its slow mocking hands, teasing my anticipation to leave. It had been a long day, and the weight of each hour had slowly climbed on my back. Five more minutes, I thought as I reached in my pocket for the gum I'd bought that morning.

For a long time, I hadn't seen the small purple gum boxes being sold, and finding them that day had been a sweet surprise. The gum's unique violet flavor was a constant treat when I was a child. I could always count on a box hiding under endless shades of lipstick and powders in my mother's purse.

I opened the box—it had the same faithful design of years before—and shook out two shiny pieces in my hand. Seeing the old familiar treats again reminded me of the days in kindergarten, which had seemed to drag as much as this day. The sweet smell of violet gum used to mark the end of those long, heavy school hours.

I'd spent the majority of my time with teachers I remember as cold and spiteful, almost childlike themselves. I'd arrive early in the morning, still adjusting to the absence of my bed. The teachers would take my hand and greet my mother with bright, sunny smiles, which disappeared when she left. For the next ten hours, they'd use their loud, demanding voices, force me to eat when I had no appetite, and hiss their impatience through every messy activity. At the end of the day, I'd ache for the tenderness of home, and my tired eyes would focus on the exit with anxious anticipation of my mother's arrival.

Finally, the door would open swiftly, and there she'd be—long brown coat, high heels clicking on the tiled floor, and a breathless smile, as if she had rushed to find me. I'd run into her arms and she'd scoop me up, allowing the weight of the day to fall to the ground. In her embrace, I'd feel the cold on her coat—the crisp air of freedom. Always there was the sweetness of her breath. The aroma of violets in her kisses at the end of such trying days made me treasure its scent long after my childhood.

I looked at the clock once again, and it was finally time to leave. I put the two pieces of gum in my mouth, then scooped up my bags and put on my long coat. As I walked through the door, the cool air felt delicious. The violets and soft wind had washed away the heaviness I'd felt just minutes before. It reminded me once again that long, tiring days always come to a sweet end.

Prayer

Lord, help me get through the tiring days that never seem to end. May the communion I share with you in devotion and prayer add sweetness to the long hours.

Controlled

✤

Train a child in the way he should go,
and when he is old he will not turn from it.

Proverbs 22:6

WHEN SHE PICKED UP the phone and heard his voice, she did her best to sound relaxed and carefree. From the moment the handsome young man at work had asked for her number, her nerves had tangled around her stomach and throat. She'd managed somehow to calm down enough to have a decent start to the conversation, but then her father walked into the room. She straightened her back and tightened the grip on the receiver as she felt the weight of her father's gaze. She tried to end the call quickly, but he was already facing her with a worried look.

"Who's on the phone?"

She covered the mouthpiece. "It's just a friend from work," she whispered.

"A boy?"

She nodded silently. He walked away and she tried to recover her voice and courage. Before she could say another word, he paced back toward the phone. "Tell him you're a Christian."

She sank into her chair. "Oh, yeah, I'm a Chris—"

"No movies. Tell him you don't go to the movies!"

Her heart started beating out of control. "Uh, yeah . . . I don't really go to the movies."

My grandfather, who became a Christian soon after my mother's conversion, grew so zealous in his faith that he strictly held on to the traditions and rules he believed came with the territory. He made certain that everyone else in the family followed the same guidelines. Going to the movies, dancing, and listening to secular music were not allowed, and dating was strictly prohibited unless a relative accompanied the couple. He was so afraid that his daughter would fall from grace by breaking the rules, he kept a tight watch.

When the painfully long and humiliating call finally ended, my mother, who was already in her twenties, remained silent, as always. Following her own conviction as an obedient Christian, she quietly did everything she was told. Although my mother's childhood was filled with moments of love and fond memories, her strict upbringing had a scarring effect. It took her years to find a voice of her own and rid herself of the insecurities and nervous timidity that weighed down on her.

In raising two daughters of her own, my mother could better relate to her father's parental fears. She could have easily controlled our every action and decided each choice that came our way. But she understood all too well how important it was just to gently guide and let us live and explore life for ourselves.

Prayer

Thank you, Lord, for the gift of free will. I want my love for you to be genuine, not programmed. Help me to remember your Word when I'm tempted to do something that might cause me harm. Thank you for giving me responsibility for my choices in life, and give me the strength to make the right ones.

TRUE WORTH

✣

*For you created my inmost being; you knit me together in my
mother's womb. I praise you because I am fearfully and wonderfully
made; your works are wonderful, I know that full well.*

PSALM 139:13–14

M Y SISTER STARED aimlessly at the flimsy gray dividers
that enclosed her into a narrow work cubicle. For five years,
she'd been sitting at the same desk in the same office chair with its
wheels going in circles. She felt trapped. The monotony of her
workday was identical to that of most women she knew. She'd arrive at 8:00 A.M. and exchange her commuter sneakers for the high
heels tucked in a bottom drawer. Pictures of the family smiled behind small glass frames as she sat stone-faced at the computer. At
noon, she'd open another drawer and reach for a can of tuna, chips,
and a box of low-fat cookies for lunch, and at five o'clock, after
hours of mindless work, she'd toss her heels back in the bottom
drawer.

It wasn't just the monotony of her workday that bothered her. For years, she'd felt belittled by her boss. He barely spoke to her, and when he did, his voice was curt and cold. She didn't have a college education, and his attitude toward her seemed to say, *You couldn't do it, even if you tried.*

That day, after lacing up her sneakers, she passed her boss in the hallway as she headed for the exit door. "Good night," she said. "Mm-hmm," he responded with a careless nod. For the first time, his rudeness slid off her back. His opinion of her didn't matter anymore. She knew what she was capable of, and starting that day, she decided to prove it.

She worked on her résumé, searched for a new job, and filled out college applications so that she could finish her education. Soon she was working for another company. Here, she felt like a valued employee—earning double the salary she had at her previous job. She proved her value every day with efficient work and then rushed to night classes four days a week.

My sister has achieved many goals she's set for herself, and she continues to live life with a fierce sense of confidence. She's no longer concerned with the conclusions of this world. Her true worth is determined by her Creator. My sister is "fearfully and wonderfully made," and she knows that full well.

Prayer

Remind me that you have created me for a purpose. Help me not to focus on what others may perceive in me, or even what I perceive in myself. Only you know my true worth and the real potential of my life. Only you can go beyond my weakness. I place my future in your hands and trust in the plans you have set for me.

BE STILL

"Be still, and know that I am God . . ."

PSALM 46:10

I WAS WAITING for a late train one afternoon, along with hundreds of others on the narrow platform. I had no book to read or music to occupy my mind. The speaker crackled and a barely audible voice announced the delay. We all strained to hear, then let out a unified grunt as we heard "twenty-minute wait." Great! I thought. Twenty more exciting minutes of looking at the littered tracks.

As I stood there, bored out of my mind, I began to look at the endless array of faces that surrounded me. In New York City, you rarely take time to look or acknowledge the people you pass. Each person is just another moving obstacle you need to dodge in order to reach your destination. This time, however, there was nowhere to go, so there I stood, looking at everyone else who had no choice but to be still. I read each face like words in a book, comparing every feature—the shapes and colors of eyes, the various bone structures, the curve of each nose, the palette of skin tones, and the colors and textures of hair. As I studied each face, this once-blurred group of New Yorkers slowly emerged one by one from the clump, revealing the art of each individual.

Although I see thousands of people each day, I'd never come to the conscious realization that each face I see is a unique, once-in-a-lifetime creation, unlike anyone other on earth. There's never been, and there will never be, another creation like yourself. I stood there in awe as I realized the detail and artistry of our wondrous Creator.

Sometimes life can feel like one big rush hour, leaving little time to reflect on the awesome glory of God and His marvelous creations. I felt as if God had held back that train just so I could remember who He truly is. When the train finally bolted through the station and the bustle of the day resumed, I thanked Him for that small moment of stillness and praised His name for the wonderful Creator He is.

Prayer

Lord, I pray the prayer of the psalmist: "When I consider your heavens, the work of your fingers, the moon and stars, which you have set in place, what is man that you are mindful of him, the son of man that you care for him?" (PSALM 8:3–4). *Thank you, Father, for the magnificence of your creations. Help me always to be mindful of your glory, and may I give you the praise and thanksgiving for all you've done.*

PLASTIC COUCHES

The house of the righteous contains great treasure...

PROVERBS 15:6

I'M ADDICTED to home-makeover programs on television. Interior designers transform rooms (in dire need of direction) into chic and elegant living spaces. As I watch, I can only imagine the miracle they could have worked on the home I grew up in—along with every other Hispanic household I'd seen in the 1980s.

Those homes all shared that trademark decor—the same colors, patterns, and items that seemed custom-made for Hispanics only. My mother's shade of choice was burgundy, but many homes had pure bright red in every area of the home—red-flowered wallpaper, red drapes, and even red wall-to-wall carpet. Green balanced out the red with plants that hung from walls and lined the windowsills. Some plants and flower arrangements were real, while others were plastic—yes, plastic, that fabulous material they couldn't live without! Practically everything was covered by a layer of plastic—couches, lamp shades, tables, and chairs. You name it, it was protected. In the summer, I'd have red marks on my legs each time I'd peel my thighs away from a chair.

The walls were a gallery of family photos in fancy frames, and there was always the glazed wooden painting of *The Last Supper*—slash clock—hanging in the living room or kitchen. Knickknacks were another trademark favorite. Little figurines with pink and light blue ribbons were kept from every wedding, baby shower, graduation, and bridal shower ever attended. Every shelf held an overpopulated community of porcelain animals, from elephants to swans, including, of course, the big red bull.

My sister and I, along with most of our cousins, are knickknack-scarred. You won't find a single figurine on any of our shelves, or much of anything else we grew up with. Through the years, my mother has changed her style, as well—although the dining room set is still covered with plastic and the couch is leather, so she can still wipe down the dust. But despite my distaste for the decor of my youth, there's much I understand and appreciate about it. Lively colors were chosen to create a bright and cheerful atmosphere. The endless figurines were cherished mementos of important events celebrated with family and friends. Couches and dining room sets were purchased with hard-earned money from humble jobs, and plastic covers protected those treasures from small sticky hands.

An interior designer could have done much to transform and improve the physical appearance of those rooms of plastic and porcelain. But when it comes to the heart of the people in the home, no redesign or improvement would have been necessary.

Prayer

Thank you, Lord, for filling my home with treasures that can't be seen. Help me always to cherish the blessings you provide. You are the designer of the heart, and I thank you for the craftsmanship and beauty you put into each one.

SALSA BLUES

There is a time for everything, and a season for every activity
under heaven: . . . a time to weep and a time to laugh,
a time to mourn and a time to dance . . .

ECCLESIASTES 3:1, 4

T HE PIANO, drums, and bongos were moving to the Latin
beat, making my shoulders and hips move to the music. "*Te
alabaré mi Dios,*" we sang, praising God in a song steeped in the
rhythm of salsa. Once the instruments were tucked away and the
church doors were closed, we'd bid our good-byes on the sidewalk.
As we'd talk and hug, "worldly" salsa would pulsate through open
car windows. Our hips, which had been shaking just minutes before, were stiff as statues now. No hip dared to budge. Our natural
sense of rhythm and movement was strictly reserved for the church
pews—the only occasion when dancing (if only just a sway) was
not considered a worldly sin.

There were exceptions, at least in my family. "Non-Christian" weddings were a real treat for me when I was growing up, because it was the only time I could ever dance. My mother reasoned that it was okay because we were with the family. That meant I had to wait for weddings, anniversaries, or birthday parties of "non-Christian" relatives. The Christians I knew didn't dance at their weddings or at any other big events. They played gospel music, ate, and played a game of hot potato to win the gaudy centerpiece.

When I truly accepted the Lord in my life at age fifteen, I struggled between my love for dancing and my love for God. Whose law was I breaking when I danced for the pure joy of dancing and not for the direct worship of God? I had never felt a direct conviction in my spirit when it came to this issue. But in the church, social dancing was always labeled "worldly"—something to be delivered from. I wasn't convinced it was wrong, and the "non-Christian" family celebrations were too far apart. So when I was eighteen years old, I took matters into my own hands and hit the clubs with my friends almost every weekend.

One night, we went to a large club where a different type of music was played on each of the four floors. The last time I had been there, we'd danced only on the disco floor. This time, however, we went upstairs to the techno room. I started dancing with my group of friends, but the mood just didn't feel right. I looked up at the stage, where men and women hired by the club were gyrating in skimpy leather thongs. A demonic-sounding voice echoed in the music, and everyone was lifting their hands and jumping up and down with crazed looks on their faces. I got an eerie chill. It felt like a satanic worship service. I couldn't dance anymore, and I told my friends I had to leave. For a long time after that night, I didn't go dancing. Maybe that was God, I told myself, confirming what everyone in church has been telling me.

As I matured in the Lord, I began meeting Christians who did not belong to my church. I was shocked when a group of these Christians invited me to go out swing dancing. I went and had an amazing time. I was spinning and twirling to the live band with my partner, and by the end of the night, we were all breathless from laughing and dancing so much. I enjoyed myself, and I knew in my heart that I'd done nothing to displease the Lord. It was a celebration of music, movement, and life.

I learned I'd have to be selective in my choice of places, and also make sure that the way I danced didn't contradict my testimony. Having a life in Christ is a learning process, and it's personal. He knows my heart and reveals to me—through discernment—those things that might be harmful. Others in their own relationship with God might have to avoid dancing completely. As an alcoholic refrains from a simple sip of wine, some people have to avoid certain environments or a mere rhythm that might take them back to a very destructive place in their lives—one they've escaped by the grace of God.

Some brothers and sisters in the Lord completely disagree with me. They might shake their heads in disappointment as they read these words. Others may silently agree but never admit it, fearful—as I used to be—that others may judge them. I would stand in front of my old church with stiff hips, when what I really wanted to do was spin and twirl to the music. But I cannot move my feet anymore according to someone else's opinion. My feet are going to move freely and dance to the rhythm God puts in my heart.

Prayer

Lord, thank you for the freedom I have in you. Help me to use that freedom wisely. In your Word, Paul says, " 'Everything is permissible for me'—but not everything is beneficial. 'Everything is permissible for me'—but I will not be mastered by anything" (1 Corinthians 6:12). Give me the discernment to know what is not beneficial for me. Help me never to put my desires ahead of you.

KNEELING ON RICE

Folly is bound up in the heart of a child,
but the rod of discipline will drive it far from him.

PROVERBS 22:15

Fathers, do not exasperate your children; instead,
bring them up in the training and instruction of the Lord.

EPHESIANS 6:4

D AD, can you please shut up!" she said, looking at him straight
in the eyes before rolling her own in disgust. My friend and
I, who were sitting at a nearby table, stopped chewing our food and
stared at each other in frozen disbelief. "Please don't speak to me
that way," he calmly responded to his eleven-year-old as she opened
and closed her hand like a talking puppet. "Blah, blah, blah," she
continued, not a tinge of worry in her eyes.

"Wow," I said as we emptied our trays into the trash and headed for the door. "Picture me saying that to my mother or father as a kid." My friend shook her head and laughed. "Are you kidding me? My mother would've whacked that little hand puppet into silence with her shoe." She took off her sandal and demonstrated with a swift sweep in air. "My mother would've just given me that look," I said, "and when we got home, it would have been over!"

Once in a while, when the topic of discipline comes up, Hispanics will get into an enthusiastic exchange of "what my mother used to do" stories. Belts and *chancletas* seemed to have been the common method for keeping one's children in check. It was usually a slap on the arm or the leg, a few more if the child did something really wrong.

Like me, many of my friends grew up in home balanced with love and discipline. I felt comfortable to speak freely with my parents, but there was a line that crossed over into disrespect. If you dared to cross that line, there were consequences. For others, crossing that line or breaking the rules resulted in consequences far more severe than the belt or the *chancleta*. Some punishments included kneeling on raw grains of rice or graters for varied amounts of time. Another required the children to hold out stones or books without letting their arms drop past a horizontal midpoint; if they did so, they were slapped. Parents, grandparents, or other family members would use tree switches, heavy shoes, or wooden paddles to strike a disobedient child. Many of these methods were considered a cultural norm. Parents believed they were doing the right thing and were often ignorant of alternative solutions.

I'm not yet a mother, and I can only imagine the struggles that accompany the joys of being a parent. Yet I'd probably raise my children like most of my family and friends do today. They openly communicate and reason with their kids, but they don't rule out a moderate spanking as a last option. I could never raise a child without consequences, unlike the father my friend and I saw eating lunch that day, but I'd never make my child kneel on a grater or strike so hard that it would leave welts. Regardless of the methods of discipline I see or learn, I hope I will be a good-enough parent to consult my Father in heaven, asking for His guidance and instruction in every situation.

Prayer

Lord, help me to be a good parent. Thank you for the examples of love and discipline you've spoken in your Word. Guide my choices, that they may benefit my children and not cause them harm.

TRUEST HIGH

Suddenly an angel of the Lord appeared and a light shone in the cell.
He struck Peter on the side and woke him up. "Quick, get up!"
he said, and the chains fell off Peter's wrists.

ACTS 12:7

MOTHER AND SON swayed to the music, tenderly holding each other on the dance floor. Josh's bride stood nearby, tears streaming down her face. All the guests were crying along with her. For over ten years, no one could have imagined this moment. The prediction was that we'd be gathered together in tears for his funeral instead.

When I was growing up, Josh, my cousins, and I all attended a Spanish Baptist church on the Lower East Side. Every Sunday, he'd attend church with his mother, but by the time he was twelve, we saw less and less of him. A few years later, his mother's tearful prayers revealed the struggles at home.

At twelve, Josh was smoking pot with his neighborhood friends, and by sixteen, his experiments with crack led him to an addiction that took over his life. He worked as a messenger, in a maintenance job, and at a clothing shop in the Village—every check filling his pockets with ten-dollar vials of crack. Each vial was a euphoric twenty-second walk in the clouds before the painful crash, and as the addiction gripped him tighter, he could no longer concentrate on work. Every thought was dedicated to the next high. In desperation for money to support his habit, he resorted to robbing people on the streets, in his family's home, and even at church.

Faithfully praying for her son, Josh's mother pleaded with the Lord for his life and visited him in rehab or prison. We all prayed as she kept us updated in church, yet I personally never envisioned change after so much time. It seemed impossible. Many of us were like the members of the first church in the New Testament who prayed fervently for Peter's release from prison. When God answered their prayer and Peter came knocking on their door, they couldn't believe it was possible. Just as with Peter, God heard a mother's fervent prayer, and after thirteen years of addiction, Josh was finally set free from drugs. Through prison ministries, he gave his life to the Lord and began a new life.

His last year in prison was dedicated to his relationship with the Lord as he studied the Word alone or in group Bible study sessions. He had a spiritual father and friend who encouraged him constantly. "God has a plan for your life," he'd say. "He's going to use you in a mighty way." Toward the end of his sentence, Josh was a worship leader and deacon of the evangelical church in prison. He was also assisting a social worker through ASAP (Alcohol and Substance Abuse Program), counseling fellow addicts.

Once released, he kept his life together with the help of the Lord, family, friends, and support services. He went from being a bag checker at a local minimarket to a position at Transitional Services for NYC, Inc. Several years and promotions later, he now serves as a supportive case manager, advocating for people with psychological, emotional, and mood disorders. In the church, he serves the Lord through music, ushering, and youth leadership. God has also placed the desire in his heart to establish a community reintegration ministry someday for newly released prisoners.

In the past, the circumstances of his addiction led me to believe it was near impossible for such a change. But as the song between mother and son came to an end on his wedding day and as friends and family wiped away tears of joy from their eyes, I was reminded to expect almost anything from such a loving and mighty God.

Prayer

Lord, you are such an awesome deliverer. Help me not to pray for others out of routine or obligation. Remind me of the power of prayer and intercession. I praise you for those who have been set free from bondage and I will continue to pray for such miracles in sincere expectation.

ALIVE

✥

*By faith in the name of Jesus, this man whom you see
and know was made strong. It is Jesus' name and the faith
that comes through him that has given this complete
healing to him, as you can all see.*

ACTS 3:16

W AVE HI," I said from behind the rented video camera. We'd
used it to tape the Easter play at church and were now visiting my father in the hospital, one week into his recovery from a quadruple bypass.

"Hi." My mother laughed. She had a bright, healthy smile and looked beautiful in her new Easter dress. She walked slowly beside my father, who looked fragile in his hospital gown.

"Oh," he said with a weak smile, pretending to be surprised, "hi, everybody." He waved gently, making the intravenous tubing sway from side to side.

I turned the camera and captured the rest of my family, who were smiling, relaxed, and making faces at the camera. I couldn't stop smiling, either. It was Easter Sunday and my father was alive.

Smiles were very different the day before his surgery. We wore tense smiles, trying hard to be optimistic. I went with him that day to check into the hospital.

"Karina, go to work," he'd pleaded that morning. "You'll see me tonight with everyone else." I went anyway, not understanding why he wanted me to go alone, or how he had convinced my mother and sister to work that day. I couldn't bear the thought of him sitting by himself, alone with fearful thoughts.

The two of us had each packed a bag that day. Mine was filled with everything I could think of that might relax and distract us—books, games, a Bible, my Walkman, and my father's favorite cassettes. I tried to fill every waiting moment, playing checkers, reading Scripture, and fitting the headset over his ears. When he wasn't listening to Pavarotti, I was desperately trying to make him laugh. Our smiles tried to convince each other that this wouldn't be our last time together.

Someone finally came to escort us to his room. It was dim and colorless. I raised the blinds as he unpacked his small bag. We had run out of things to say. Our smiles were less broad and less convincing. A doctor walked in and sat next to Papi. She introduced herself in a soothing voice and then proceeded to explain the operation in full detail—the incisions, the sawing through bones, the metal clamp, and the machines that would pump his heart and breathe for his lungs. I didn't react. For weeks, we knew what the operation would entail. Yet as she finished, Papi's wide eyes, which had been looking straight at her the whole time, began to well up with tears.

"I know this is hard," she said, putting her hand on his shoulder. He nodded in silence, his tears not yet falling, but rising in his eyes.

I almost didn't want her to leave. Her presence was like a dam holding back a flood of tears from my father and me. I rushed toward him as she walked out of the door. We held each other and cried in a way that sounded almost foreign. I realized then why he'd tried to convince me not to come. He wanted the freedom to express his fear without worrying me.

Worry and sadness passed. That Easter Sunday as we taped one another's joy, we gave thanks to the Lord for hearing our prayers. We walked back to the once-colorless room, which was now filled with bright balloons, flowers, and get-well cards. It was no longer a tomb, but a celebration of life.

Prayer

Lord, lift up families who are dealing with the illness of a loved one. Give them strength, unity, and, most of all, peace. I thank you for the countless testimonies of healing, and I will trust in your mercy and power when my life is confronted with sickness.

Mami and Papi:
A Love Story

✛

*He who finds a wife finds what is good
and receives favor from the LORD.*

Proverbs 18:22

IT WAS LABOR DAY weekend and the congregation slowly filled
the bus that would take them to the church picnic. A beautiful
young woman sat near the window, anxiously saving the empty
seat next to her. Her aunt walked through the narrow aisle with
her heavy bags and plopped down next to her.

"You can't sit here," the young woman said in a panic. "It's taken."

She continued to guard the seat until the handsome young man
she was waiting for finally came on board. "Geño," she said with a
smile, "sit here."

As he sat down, he tried to convince himself this momentary joy
meant nothing. She's just being friendly, you fool, he said to himself. That's all. He'd worked so hard to bury his secret admiration

for the preacher's daughter. She spoke perfect English and held a secretarial position—something he considered very high-class. Convinced of his unworthiness, he had left New York to forget her. When he returned years later, he was certain the crush was over. But now they were sitting together at her request, and his heart was drumming out of control.

Once they arrived at the picnic area, she invited him to her family's table and served him the food she'd prepared with her mother. At the beach, she picked up seaweed and threw it at him as she laughed and smiled. He played along, laughing and throwing it back, but his mind was a tangle of confusion and doubt. Can this possibly mean what I think it means? he wondered.

He rushed to his brother for advice. "Ruperto, she threw seaweed at me!" After hearing the whole situation, my uncle blurted, "*Sangano*, what are you waiting for! Just tell her how you feel already!"

On the bus back, they sat next to each other again. He looked at my mother and finally said it: "Connie, I like you very much. What do you think my chances are? Do you have any feelings for me?"

After a moment of sheer joy and terror, my mother responded, "Let's try."

Everyone on the bus had already begun singing *coritos*. She opened her songbook and they each held one side, their nervous hands shaking the book the whole way home.

Prayer

Thank you, Lord, for those who find each other in love. Keep making these introductions. Bless those in new relationships. Strengthen their foundation and guide their choices for the future.

A LIFE WORTH LIVING

In the same way, the Spirit helps us in our weakness.
We do not know what we ought to pray for, but the Spirit himself
intercedes for us with groans that words cannot express.

ROMANS 8:26

I ALWAYS HAD a dull pain in my stomach from anxiety whenever my parents drove me to junior high school. The school building, small in the distance, would get bigger and bigger, like a growing monster, until the car stopped at the entrance gate. "Bye," I'd grunt in a barely audible voice.

"Have a nice day," my mother would chirp, all sun and smiles. They'd drive away and there I'd stand—thirteen and the perfect picture of awkward adolescence.

I was practically blind, and the glasses I wore made sure everyone knew it. The frames were huge and the lenses thick and heavy, leaving an ever-present red indentation on my nose. My mouth was a sloppy mess of orthodontal work; dull silver rings surrounded each tooth and a hardened ooze of cement lay below each one. My face was still trying to grow into my nose, and my hair wasn't doing me any favors, either. Basically, I was a geek.

Unfortunately, I wasn't even a smart geek. The smart ones were put in a class together, where they could be awkward in peace. I, on the other hand, got stuck with the dreaded general population. My class was made up of break-dancer wannabes, girls with fat gold earrings and bright red lips, and other girls who seemed bigger and tougher than most of the boys. The teacher would stand in front of the class, basically talking to the blackboard, while the students carried on noisily, spitting soggy sunflower-seed shells on the ground. I had two friends in my class, and when they were absent, I didn't speak the whole day. The fight culture was big, and I saw enough fights to keep me in a constant state of paranoia. I swallowed any snide comments made at my expense. I didn't want to be on the opposite side of girls who'd smear Vaseline on their faces and file their nails into arrow-shaped daggers before a fight.

In addition to my school blues, life from the age of twelve to fourteen was filled with a constant gloom. My sister was beautiful and confident and wore all the right clothes. Next to her, I felt cheated. My mother and I loved to take our frustrations out on each other. We argued all the time, and hearing her loud high heels coming up the hallway stairs made me cringe. The highlight of my day was after school, when no one was home. I'd load up on a ridiculous amount of junk food and devour it while I watched TV. My level of boredom, insecurity, and loneliness was so profound at that time that there was even a moment on my cousin's twelfth-floor balcony when I wished I had the courage to just jump off.

As I look back now, I think that God allowed those two years of deep sadness in order to plant in me a real love and understanding for young people. Most of their problems go above and beyond the problems I had faced. Despite the tension between my mother and me, she honestly loved me, and I had the support of the rest of my family. Some kids have to deal with adolescence and depression without the love of family.

Regardless how or when you get there, depression is a real place. Once there, it feels like you'll never leave. I, however, can testify to the fact that there's a way out. As I go through the photo albums now and see that sad little girl, I wish I could have told her what I can now tell others—that one day she'd break away from that dark temporary shell and go on to have a beautiful life worth living.

Prayer

Lord, thank you for the promise that the Holy Spirit will always help us in our times of weakness. When I cannot quite find the words to pray, intercede on my behalf with the words I cannot express. Thank you for bringing me through the seasons of my life and allowing me to become the fulfilled person you want me to be.

REMEDIES

I DON'T HAVE TO SEE the *tilo* leaves boiling in a pot of bubbling water. The herbal scent fills the house and testifies to my father's pain. "Your stomach again?" I ask, watching him pour the caramel-colored tea through a strainer. Forget chalky spoonfuls of Mylanta or Pepto-Bismol. My father's been soothing his aches and pains with herbs since he was a little boy in Puerto Rico.

Living with limited means and far away from pill-popping Western culture, people learned to use the resources around them to ease their ailments. Plants and flowers, oil, mud, and fruits and vegetables replaced bottles of bitter syrup and prescription pills. Among the many medicinal herbs are shine bush (*la paletaria*), ideal for heat rash, other skin irritations, and bladder problems; lemon balm *(el toronjil)* and Caribbean spearmint *(la yerba buena)*, both good for stomach pains, nausea, and vomiting. These were medicines of generations past. Even now in the United States, many Hispanics are reluctant to swallow doctor-recommended drugs without first trying an alternative solution.

Stomachaches in my house were treated with teas, of course, but another popular antidote was warm olive oil with a bit of salt. My mother would mix the two in her hand, rub my stomach, and say a prayer. Another popular remedy was rubbing alcohol. I don't think there's one Hispanic I know who didn't have an alcohol rub-down as a kid. When you were burning up with fever, out came a bowl of ice-cold water mixed with alcohol and a portable fan on a chair. After being massaged with the cool, damp washcloth, the brisk wind of the fan would huff, puff, and blow that fever away.

Then there are the bizarre remedies, the "Are you sure you want to do that?" ones—for example, a few drops of fresh baby urine in your ear for an earache, or a drop of cool black coffee in your eye when it's infected. Are your limbs a little swollen? Strip down those green plantains and place the slimy peels on your problem area. Apparently, the peels pull the fluid right out, and, hey, when you're done, you can fry up those naked plantains for dinner. Money works, too! A penny on the forehead is said to take away a bloody nose, and a quarter smeared with a little butter and pressed on a bump takes that *chicon* down to size.

But the hands-down favorite in practically all Hispanic households is the miracle goop of all time—Vicks VapoRub! My sister and I were slathered with that stuff every time we sneezed. Just like my father's *tilo* tea, its strong smell announced "somebody's sick!" as soon as you'd walk through the door. It doesn't exactly fit with the natural remedies imported from the *campo*, but we like it just the same.

Our ancestors, who passed down these natural cures, didn't always have the option to see a doctor and get a prescription as we can now; they used God's organic creations to ease their suffering. And although we have the advantages of the modern world, I'm thankful for wonderful remedies born out of necessity in another time.

Prayer

Lord, in your word you speak of those who were healed with herbs, wine, oil, and mud (EZEKIAL 47:12; I TIMOTHY 5:23; ISAIAH 1:6; JOHN 9:6). *Yet in each case, your power was the source of the healing. Thank you for simple remedies, as well as the advances in medicine, but above all, I rely on you, Lord, my healer and my deliverer.*

PEEL

When the perishable has been clothed with the imperishable, and the mortal with immortality, then the saying that is written will come true: "Death has been swallowed up in victory. Where, O death, is your victory? Where, O death, is your sting?"

1 CORINTHIANS 15:54–55

WHENEVER I SLEPT over at my grandparents' home, I'd wake to the smell of breakfast and the sound of pots sizzling. I'd shuffle over to the kitchen, give Alela and Pápa a sleepy hug, and settle into a chair. It was always me and Pápa at the table as my grandmother fussed over the food and coffee. Most of my memories are of him in his wheelchair, sitting beside me in the kitchen. We'd talk and eat our eggs the same way—piercing the dome of our eggs over easy and sponging the puddle of yoke with bread.

When Alela took away our plates, my grandfather would reach into the bowl of fruit. He always ate fruit with a knife in his hands, sculpting pieces of apple, then eating the smooth slices he'd cut and passing me some. Pápa would peel an orange by turning it carefully in his hands and making an even ribbon that curled away from the fruit in one continuous strand. After breakfast, he'd read the newspaper and give me the comics section. We'd sit there quietly, and I'd interrupt his reading only to show him the really funny jokes.

Those quiet moments I shared with my grandfather were sandwiched between the active life of his past and the terrible illness of his future. This published poet, gifted pianist, and fervent preacher spent the last years of his life in pain, confined to a bed. The color of his vibrant life slowly edged away, like the bright oranges he used to peel, until his pale and pain-ridden body came to a rest. My only consolation as the family gathered together in the funeral home were the three white doves and the words etched into the fabric lining of the casket. They read "Going Home." Instead of focusing on my grandfather's death, I imagined his new life in heaven, and his vibrant spirit, untouched by the hands of death.

> *An old*
> > *man*
> *sat in*
> > *his chair*
> *peeling*
> > *an orange.*
> *As he*
> > *turned*
> *the sphere*
> > *in his hands,*

a bright
  ribbon edged
its way
    toward
the ground,
      until this fruit,
once the color
    of the sun,
sat bare
    and pale
in his hands.

Prayer

When the years of my life peel away, it may appear to be the end, but you've placed a living soul beneath my skin, one that never dies. I thank you, Lord, not for an end, but for a new beginning with you— when the sweetness and the heart of who I truly am will emerge from within.

A Distant Life

He heals the brokenhearted and binds up their wounds.

PSALM 147:3

T HE PLANE was slowly descending. Melinda could now see the landscape of the country that had taken so much away from her. As a child, she had dreamed of this faraway land and envisioned embracing her father once again. He had left Peru eight years before and had convinced the tearful little girl he would return soon and take the family to this land of dreams. Yet after years of letters—which filled several boxes—she'd begun to lose hope.

He'd been gone for four years when her mother gathered the children to read the latest letter. Her hands began to shake as she read it out loud. This was the letter they'd been waiting for. He was ready for them to join him in America! Melinda listened with joy and excitement. But suddenly, her mother stopped reading. Her face seemed to freeze, except for her eyes, which moved frantically over the words. There wasn't enough money for everyone to travel to America just yet. Melinda and her sister would have to stay behind.

This mysterious land of dreams was a thief that had taken away her father, and it was now taking her mother and siblings. Although they'd promised to send for her and her sister as soon as they could, she no longer waited with the hope of a child. The two girls moved in with their aunt, but Melinda felt like an orphan.

Melinda had no choice but to accept the life she'd been given, and by the age of sixteen she'd created a life she was content with. She had many friends, a steady boyfriend, and was finishing high school. It was then she received the letter she'd been waiting for all this time—but one she no longer desired. She now had to say good-bye to her life in Peru and start over in a strange country with a family she barely knew anymore.

As the plane safely landed, everyone was clapping except Melinda. Why now? she thought. Where was this moment when I really needed it?

Once outside, she was greeted with icy wind and a strange white landscape, one of many shocking new experiences yet to come in America. The cabdriver dropped them in front of the funeral home, where the family was living and working in exchange for a small salary and rent-free housing. She stood in the snow, looking at this house of death, frozen and seemingly lifeless herself.

The family reunion was rich with tears of joy, resentment, and fear. Melinda hugged her father with the longing she'd felt as an eight-year-old, but in her thoughts, she was holding a stranger. Her little brother, whom she'd cared for and loved so deeply in Peru, looked at her with distant eyes. He clung to his other sister, not sure what to think about these two new girls who claimed to be his sisters, as well.

As much as her parents tried to make them feel welcome, it was hard not to feel like a guest in someone else's home. The adjustment within the family was challenging; there was another language to learn, a new school to survive in, and mandatory work at home—cleaning chapels filled with flowers and corpses.

From the time her father left Peru to her early years in America, she could never have imagined the life she enjoys today. Her loneliness has been replaced by the security of a loving husband, and in exchange for the years of instability, she now has a home she can call her own. Yet the most cherished difference is the intimacy and love she now shares with her parents and siblings. The old wounds are healed and those ancient fears are memories she shares with me over coffee on the porch of her sister (my cousin's wife). "It's been a long journey," she says, smiling as she listens to the voices and laughter of her family in the background, "but I'm finally home."

Prayer

Father, I pray for the many people who struggle to find a place for themselves and their families. Many have no choice but to accept the life they've been given. For others, the promise of a new life is fraught with strange customs and new challenges. I thank you for the testimonies of those who've struggled yet persevered. Thank you for healing their broken hearts and binding up their wounds.

YOUTH RETREAT

I love those who love me, and those who seek me find me.

PROVERBS 8:17

¡GLORIA A DIOS, amen!" the pastor shouted from the pulpit once again. My cousin and I looked at each other, quietly giggled, and whispered, "Twenty-three." Keeping track of the preacher's compulsive habits were just one of the many ways we got through the long Sunday sermons. Others including coloring, passing silly notes, and sneaking to the other room to play an assortment of games, from Mother May I to Red Light, Green Light.

Sunday mornings were long enough, but then there were Sunday evening services, which lasted just as long. In between services, we'd go to my grandmother's house for the ritual feast, and then my sister and I would beg my mother to let us stay there while they went to church. "Please, Mami," we'd whine, tugging on her clothes and making an assortment of pathetic faces. "Pleeeeeeeeease!" Sometimes we'd shout for joy, then change into our pajamas and cuddle on the couch with my aunt and cousin for a night of movies. Yet most times we'd pout behind our parents as we headed out the door toward the car. "It's not fair," I'd hiss under my breath.

This was how I felt about the Lord and His day until I was fifteen years old. My feelings changed the weekend I went away for my first youth retreat. Our church had recently joined the American Baptist Churches Association, and we were now building relationships with other churches in New York City. Youth from these different churches were going to Pennsylvania for a three-day retreat.

I was so excited! There would be swimming, games, hiking, and fresh air! We boarded the bus with our backpacks and brown paper bags filled with goodies, then cheered as the bus began to move. We drove past the graffiti-clad buildings and tall skyscrapers, until soon we were surrounded by trees and green hills.

"Cows!" someone shouted on the left side of the bus.

"Wow!" we screamed, piling toward the windows on the left side for a better look at this rare sight. We were all thrilled to get out of the city, away from our parents, and for me, it was an opportunity to get away from my boring church.

The weekend proved to be as much fun as I'd thought it would be, but I received so much more than I'd imagined. Besides the interesting activities, I met so many new people, and these relationships changed my life. Each person had a different story, but whether they'd been raised in the church or had just started going recently, they all seemed to have a special relationship with God. I knew Him only in a matter-of-fact way, like reading about George Washington in a history book. They, on the other hand, were speaking about Him as if He were actively present in their lives.

This was new to me, and because they were my age, they had my attention.

At one point during the retreat, the leaders encouraged us to have some quiet time with the Lord. It sounded a bit strange to me, but I agreed and found a private spot on the bank of a stream. I started to pray, but it wasn't the mechanical "Dear heavenly Father" I'd recited all my life. I just talked to Him. The red and brown leaves fell softly all around me, landing gently on the ground and water, and as I sat there, I felt God's presence fall upon me with the same tenderness as those leaves.

That last night, there was a concert, and the music drenched my spirit with an indescribable joy. I now understood the relationship the others had with the Lord. For the first time in my life, He was more than just a name. Since that time, God has continued to be the center of my life. It's not every day I feel the tight connection or emotional bond I felt that weekend, but regardless of how I feel from one day to the next, I know God is real and ever present in my life.

If what I'm saying are simply words on a page to you, or if God is only a name or religious icon, I dare you to go below the surface. Take just a moment to be alone with God and talk to Him honestly and openly. See if God won't reveal the true nature and power of His existence through Jesus Christ. As I learned so many years ago, you can never fully understand this until you've experienced it for yourself.

Prayer

Father, thank you for revealing yourself to those who seek you with a sincere heart. Lord, today I invite your presence so that I may draw close to you. I want to feel your presence and truly know you in a personal way.

MOVING IN

In my Father's house are many rooms; if it were not so,
I would have told you. I am going there to prepare a place for you.
And if I go and prepare a place for you, I will come back and take
you to be with me that you also may be where I am.

JOHN 14:2–3

W HILE MY PARENTS planned their wedding, they searched for a place to raise their future family. After months of searching, they found a good-size apartment for a reasonable price in a quiet Brooklyn neighborhood. The landlord, who'd first shown the apartment to my light-skinned mother, was shocked to hear my father's thick Spanish accent.

"Oh," he gasped, "you're Hispanic?"

My mother gave him a knowing smile. "Yes, we are."

As they completed the paperwork, he did his best to discourage my parents. "I don't want to scare you or anything, but this area is a bit prejudiced. It might not be the right place for you to live."

My mother signed on the dotted line, then handed the pen over to my father. "Thanks for the warning. We'll be just fine."

My parents proved to be good tenants and respectable neighbors, but there were occasional incidents. The landlord had been right about the prejudice we'd face, but most of it came from him and his family, who lived just below us. Despite the fact that my parents made us tiptoe after 9:00 P.M., there were complaints about "the noise." Sometimes his wife would get bold and throw in a few racist comments.

My parents handled this ignorance with wisdom, care, and lots of prayer. Despite the problems with our landlord and the stress it caused, I enjoyed my neighborhood. I had plenty of friends, and the majority of our neighbors proved to be wonderful families and never gave us any grief. There were negative moments of verbal harassment by a group of kids who called me "spick," but that was short-lived. For the most part, my memories are positive. Even our landlord eased up after we had lived there for many years.

Before we arrived, there might have been a looming sense of racism in the neighborhood. It's possible that many people there had never even known a Hispanic family before we moved in. It's easy to assume the validity of stereotypes if you've never been exposed to someone from a particular ethnic group. My neighbors may have entertained misconceptions at first, but they learned we were just another family, like every other family on the block.

Prayer

Father, protect those who are held down, cheated, and mistreated by racism. I pray you give them strength and wisdom to work through their situations. Lord, forgive those who do not practice hospitality toward all, but instead harbor racist attitudes. I pray that you might heal the source of their hate and mistrust.

MAKING COFFEE

✠

I always thank God for you because of his grace given you in
Christ Jesus. For in him you have been enriched in every way . . .

1 CORINTHIANS 1:4–5

MY BROTHER and I looked at the selection of choices on the red-and-cream sign above us—caramel macchiato, white choco mocha, vanilla latte. The list went on and on. I ordered a hot chocolate and my brother got the simplest cup of coffee the fancy New York shop could offer.

I looked around as we waited by the counter. It seemed we were the only ones there for the purpose of relaxation and companionship. Customers with stressed eyes bolted out the door with their drinks, while others sat alone, busy with their books, laptops, and stacks of paper.

We chose a small table near the window. Having been raised apart, we were happy to sit together for a rare moment to catch up.

My brother took the first sip of his coffee, then smiled as he shook his head. "It's funny," he said, "almost five dollars for this coffee, and it doesn't even come close to the coffee we made fresh in Puerto Rico."

I held the warm cup in my hands, anticipating a story from his childhood—my only window into a life we didn't share. My half brother and sister were mainly raised by their grandmother in Puerto Rico. From the stories I'd already heard, I know the life they'd shared had not always been easy, or even pleasant. Yet this memory of making coffee with his grandmother brought a smile to his face as he spoke.

"We grew the coffee beans right on our land," he began. "All the grandkids would pick coffee beans with my grandmother and put them into a huge cloth sack." He took the little wooden stirring stick from his coffee and gestured as he spoke. "We'd get these big wooden sticks and beat the bag of coffee beans to loosen the husks around them. Ah," he said, closing his eyes and taking a deep breath through his nose, "that's when you'd begin to smell the aroma of the coffee. It was such a rich smell. After that, we'd put handfuls of coffee beans on big round plates. We would toss the beans into the air and blow out the husks." He blew into the air as if he were blowing out birthday candles. "That was the fun part." "We had a homemade wooden stove, and we'd put the coffee beans in a big old black cauldron, where they would begin to roast over the fire. Little by little, we'd pour in white sugar. When the mixture was finally ground, we'd put it into a cone-shaped cloth and pour boiling water through it."

He took another sip of his coffee from the paper cup and smiled once more. "What a difference from how I get my coffee now. But the best part was when we finally drank it . . . how we drank it . . .

together. It wasn't what you see here, taking coffee to go, rushing from one place to the other. The time we spent together drinking coffee was almost sacred. I'd sit there with my buttered bread on the cool tiles of the living room floor, or around the kitchen table, and we'd just talk for hours. My grandmother would tell us stories of when she was a little girl, or we'd read her verses from the Bible by the light of oil lamps."

As I listened to my brother's story, I could just taste how delicious the whole experience must have been. I didn't grow up drinking coffee and don't enjoy the taste now, but how wonderful it would have been to spend the day making coffee with my brother and sister, to sit with them on cool tiles and talk for hours. While that was never meant to be, the small amount of time we spend together now is as sacred as my brother's memory of his grandmother and the times they shared together so many years ago.

Prayer

Lord, thank you for the fellowship I enjoy with my loved ones, and the memories that follow. Help me to cherish the small moments with those dear to my heart. For those who live far from me, help me to remember them through letters, phone calls, and prayers lifted up to you.

No English

But he said to me, "My grace is sufficient for you,
for my power is made perfect in weakness." . . .

2 Corinthians 12:9

ANGELICA CLUTCHED the hands of her children as they ex-
ited the plane. She searched the crowd of strangers with
wide, desperate eyes. What if something had happened to him?
Who would help her find him, and how would she even ask?
These worries had been tormenting her since she'd said good-bye
to her family in Colombia and boarded the plane to America, the
place her husband had spent three long years preparing their
new life.

"Angelica!" She saw her husband and ran to him, no longer
afraid. She clung to him in relief, then, like a child, took his hand
and let him lead the way.

The transition proved easier than she'd expected. Her new home in Miami, Florida, was a Hispanic community where shopkeepers all spoke Spanish and sold familiar products. Spanish was spoken in the streets and on television at home. In the midst of such life-changing circumstances, it was comforting to know she didn't have to adjust to her new life in a language she didn't speak. While her husband, who spoke English fairly well, supported the family, she took care of the home and eased into the comfort of her environment. Her children struggled with challenges she didn't have to face. Confused, terrified, and out of place, they'd sit in their new classrooms mute and powerless, listening day by day to these strange new sounds.

Eight years later, the children's English had improved, though they continued to communicate in Spanish at home with their parents. Communication between husband and wife, however, had soured, and the couple eventually separated. Angelica moved for the second time in her life, boarding a plane with her children to start a new life in New York City.

She faced the challenge of supporting her children without her husband for the first time. With it came the other challenge she'd been able to avoid previously—the language barrier. She experienced the voiceless fear her children had faced years ago when they began school. She looked for work with gestures, exaggerated facial expressions, and broken English as she struggled for a way to establish a secure home for her kids.

She eventually found work as a housekeeper for two kind families, who encouraged her to improve her English. One family, sympathetic to her embarrassment at speaking English, offered to pay for language courses. She gratefully accepted and began classes two days a week after work. She struggled to balance work, her children, and home responsibilities with her new lessons, but it proved too much to handle. She had to give up her classes.

Because she has lived in Hispanic communities (both in Miami and New York) and has had little time to learn properly, Angelica remains uncomfortable with English after eighteen years in the United States. This might be hard to believe or accept for those raised in this country, but many Hispanics who arrive here later in life can relate to Angelica's plight. Leaving a familiar life in order to build a new one in another country is filled with plenty of challenges. If one can survive using the language one knows, learning another can take a backseat to the immediate needs of survival. Of course, there are those who have plenty of time and resources but don't give a second thought to learning English. But not every non-English speaker in America fits this category.

Now that Angelica's children are grown and the burdens of responsibility are less, she's looking forward to going back to her English classes. She's determined to speak English well, if only to converse with her American-born grandchildren—children who'll have a fresh start, thanks to their grandmother, who paved the way.

Prayer

Lord, help me be a bridge for those who struggle with transitions and language barriers. Even if I don't know their language, show me how to communicate beyond words by offering love and kindness. In the same way, let me be a bridge to those who don't know you. For many, a relationship with you is something foreign and new. Send me to communicate your glory.

LETHAL LEGALISM

*". . . 'These people honor me with their lips, but their hearts are far
from me. They worship me in vain; their teachings are but rules
taught by men.' You have let go of the commands of God
and are holding on to the traditions of men."*

MARK 7:6–8

A T THE AGE OF NINE, my friend Lara watched her mother
throw out all her jeans and slacks. She couldn't understand
what was going on. What had happened to her parents, and why
was God telling them to throw away her pants? After her family
joined a new church, they replaced the clothes in her closet with
long skirts—what "respectable Christian girls" wore. There were
other changes: Her mother's once-shiny red lips were now wiped
pale, her long painted fingernails were clipped and bare, and her
jewelry remained in its boxes. This was Lara's first introduction to
God—a fearful old man constantly preoccupied with wardrobe.

Every morning, Lara would dress herself in clothes she hadn't chosen, and in the same way she'd dress every part of her outward being in order to appear righteous. She learned to conform to the rules and create an outer illusion that met the expectations of her parents and the church. No one bothered to look beyond her facade. If they had, they would have seen the decay of her spirit, and the emptiness and confusion that consumed her.

Growing up, she had no free will or voice of her own, and, worse than that, she never learned to develop an honest and personal relationship with Christ. All she learned was what the church expected of her. The long list of dos and don'ts engulfed her life, but she honestly believed that rejecting the legalistic mask meant rejecting God Himself.

In addition to being spiritually stifled, she was surrounded by hypocrisy. The artificial masks of many began to crack in her presence, revealing the truth of their natures, which were evidently untouched by the true Spirit of the living God. Lara had had enough. She disconnected herself completely from what she believed to be God's world and lost all trust for anything associated with Him. She ripped off her mask and set out to fill her empty spirit by any means possible. She indulged herself with every forbidden fruit she could possibly reach, and binged on all the don'ts she'd grown up with. Yet regardless of what she did, or how she tried to fill the void, her spirit remained empty.

After years of futile searching, Lara prayed a very real and honest prayer: Lord, if you really exist, please show me. If I serve you, I want to serve you the way you intended, not the way man intended. God heard her prayer and began breathing life into her dead soul. It was refreshing and light, unlike anything she'd ever experienced.

Years before, her parents had attempted to introduce her to God by changing her wardrobe. Yet the day she truly met Him was the day she asked Him to transform her soul.

Prayer

As a balloon filled with human breath will never rise from the ground, so my life will be if I rely merely on my own strength. Lord, fill me with your Spirit so that I may experience life more abundantly and rise to my full potential. As helium gives the balloon its flight, let me soar with your breath of life.

THE AMERICAN
DREAM HOME

✢

For he was looking forward to the city with foundations,
whose architect and builder is God.

HEBREWS 11:10

T HE AMERICAN DREAM is to have a big house in the suburbs
with lots of rooms. The girl's room is pink, with a Barbie-
print quilt, and the boy's room blue, filled with toy dinosaurs,
Tonka trucks, and a KEEP OUT sign on the door. It's the house I
grew up watching on TV. Yet the space I actually grew up in was
very different.

The place my parents moved into after they were married was a
long railroad apartment in Brooklyn. If you've never heard of a railroad apartment, just picture the equivalent of a wide train with
the connecting doors between cars missing. In ours, you'd walk
through the kitchen, two bedrooms (divided by a short, narrow
hallway), and a room of dressers to reach the caboose of the living

room. The only room with four walls was the bathroom, our only place of solitude. There weren't many opportunities to be alone and shut yourself away from the rest of the family.

Regardless of the obvious inconveniences and lack of privacy and space, I can honestly say that I loved my home. The small space seemed to embrace us and bring us closer together, and it's where some of my most cherished memories took place. We had no choice but to work out problems, communicate, and enjoy one another's company.

I sometimes try to imagine how these memories would change if I had grown up in an American dream house, which for many seems so important to obtain. I envision us pulling away from one another, up stairwells, through hallways, until we're all shut away in our rooms in silence.

I understand the difference between a house and a home. Wherever I will raise my family, the size of the space and the number of rooms will never be a symbol of our failure or success as a family. My American dream home is one that God will fill with as much love, laughter, and closeness as I experienced in our small railroad apartment in Brooklyn.

Prayer

Lord, I know that a home is much more than the living space that surrounds me. Thank you for the love of family and the anointing of your Spirit, those things that make a house a home.

ARMPIT DELIVERY

✥

"Which of you, if his son asks for bread, will give him a stone?
Or if he asks for a fish, will give him a snake?"

MATTHEW 7:9–10

MOTHER AND DAUGHTER were on their way home from visiting a relative and her newborn in the hospital. As they boarded the bus, the excited sixteen-year-old began talking about the miracle of giving birth. "Mami," she said with wonderment, "isn't it amazing how a baby so big can come out of a space so small?"

The mother's eyes widened, then whipped around to face her daughter. "What?" she shrieked. "What are you talking about? Who told you that?" The embarrassed teenager looked around at the other passengers, who were beginning to stare.

"*De aquí,*" the mother continued, lifting her hand in the air and pointing to her underarm. "They come from here!"

This woman was my grandmother, trying frantically to keep my mother in the dark. Ironically, she named my mother Concepcíon, yet never talked with her about sex. My Puerto Rican grandmother had been raised in the *campo*, where menstruation, sex, and giving birth were shameful secrets you figured out on your own. Although her daughters grew up in America, she raised them as she'd been brought up in Puerto Rico.

My mother and her sister often learned of these "shameful" subjects in embarrassing situations, where their ignorance stood out for all to see. My mother used to shriek "No!" when asked if she was a virgin. She wasn't sexually active, but she had no idea what the word *virgin* meant. She thought it was a part of the Holy Mother's name. She assumed they were asking if she thought she was holy like the Virgin Mary. "Why does everyone ask if I'm a virgin? I'm not fanatic, holier than thou, praying all the time!" she'd say.

Their lessons in sex education were humiliating. "She kept us naïve," my aunt tells me, a tinge of resentment still in her voice. "We walked around like ignorant fools."

When it came to discussing sex, my mother did the opposite of what my grandmother had done. We asked her the big question relatively young, but she didn't shy away. According to her, if we were old enough to ask, we were old enough to know. She sat us down with library books and gave simple, truthful answers to all our questions. It was important that her children not experience the same embarrassment she had, because growing up in ignorance was anything but bliss.

Prayer

Lord, you communicate truth to those you have created. Help those who find it difficult to share reality and truth with those who depend on them. I thank you for the wonderful miracles in my body. Let me not be ashamed of the natural wonders you've created in me.

ACCENTS

Therefore encourage one another and build each other up,
just as in fact you are doing.

THOUSAND!" she blurts out, interrupting her sister's conversation with me.

We both turn and look at her with the same "Excuse me?" expression in our eyes.

"Thousand," she repeats, that "little sister" smirk on her face, "not towsand." She returns her attention to the television, a mischievous smile of satisfaction on her face.

"Thhhhhhhousand!" my friend spits out, her tongue halfway out of her mouth.

They're fifteen years apart, and the younger one, who was born and raised in America, has no trace of her big sister's Spanish accent.

"Okay, now it's your turn," my friend says, victory already spelled out in her face. *"Rápido corren los carros cargados de azucar en el ferro-carril."* She rolls each *r* with a force that seems to jab her little sister into a fetal position.

"All right!" her sister responds with a fit of laughter, as if she's just been tickled mercilessly. "All right, I won't say another word."

The sisters smile, calling a temporary truce. This kind of mockery between them is nothing new. They constantly challenge and correct each other's pronunciation, but no one ever walks away truly offended. It's all in fun, and their love would never let it reach a harsher level. My friend had already experienced that kind of cruel torment when she moved to America from Colombia at the age of eleven.

Learning a new language so late was like the experience of recovering from a stroke. She had to relearn how to function in her environment from scratch, regressing to the level of a toddler. For each word, she'd awkwardly wrestle with the muscles in her mouth as she tried to pronounce the new sounds. Many of her schoolmates made the process even tougher, for they ridiculed her relentlessly with cruel words and imitations.

Speaking with her years later in her living room, I hear that her Spanish accent is still present, but there is no longer any shame attached to it. Although some were cruel, others encouraged her, helping her combat her insecurities, which were as thick as her accent. They corrected her with kindness and applauded her improvements until she gained confidence. She continues to improve her pronunciation, and she welcomes those willing to point out her mistakes—even her little sister.

Prayer

Regardless of how I sound when I speak, I pray that the words I say are pleasing to you. Help me to build others up with words of kindness and encouragement.

NOT JUST BUTTER PECAN

From one man he made every nation of men,
that they should inhabit the whole earth . . .

ACTS 17:26

IN MY FAMILY, I have relatives with strong African roots and
those whose features reveal a connection to European ancestors.
The image a lot of people think of when they hear the word *His-*
panic is what my mother likes to call "butter pecan"—someone
with café con leche skin, as well as wavy dark brown hair. Hispanics who don't fall into that middle ground are sometimes mistaken
to be of a different ethnic origin. Having "non-Hispanic" features
can sometimes mask one's true identity and create some interesting situations.

The relatives on my mother's side of the family are mostly fair-
skinned and have light hair and eyes that are blue, green, or soft
brown. Most people are shocked when they hear them speaking

Spanish for the first time. "You're Hispanic?" they ask, their eyes wide with shock. "I would never have guessed." These people may walk away a bit surprised, but that's nothing compared to those who have to squirm away with the taste of their foot in their mouth.

One such episode occurred when my mother was on her way home from work. She was waiting for the train when a coworker approached her on the platform. He worked in a different department, so their communication until then had been limited to brief hellos. When the train arrived, they found seats together and started off with small talk. Somehow, the conversation found its way to the subject of tax deductions on their paychecks, and that's when the foot chewing began.

"It's a shame that people like you and I have to work all day," he complained, "while these Puerto Ricans on welfare sit around collecting our hard-earned money." My mother, who had been in this situation before, decided to keep her mouth shut and let him ramble on. Of course he did, knocking Puerto Ricans the entire train ride from Manhattan to Brooklyn. My mother smiled and nodded her head, just waiting for her moment. When the train was two stops away from her station, she hit him with the question. "What nationality are you?" she asked with a smile.

"Irish," he responded.

"Oh . . . Guess what nationality I am."

He turned his body toward her, excited about the little guessing game. "Let's see." He looked carefully at her light yellow-brown eyes, white skin, and dark blond hair. "Polish," he said, content with his answer.

"Nope. Try again."

He went down the list from German to Australian, growing a

bit frustrated. When the train was just about to pull into her station, he gave up. "Okay, tell me. What nationality *are* you?"

Her smile was wide and full of satisfaction. "I'm Puerto Rican."

The loud train screeched to a halt. His face froze. "Oh . . . uh . . . well . . . I didn't mean *all* Puerto Ricans. . . . I . . ."

She calmly walked through the open doors and flicked her wrist as if shooing away a mosquito. "Good-bye."

In short, with all the varieties that make up the Hispanic community, it's important to remember that we come in a lot more flavors than just butter pecan.

Prayer

Do not answer a fool according to his folly, or you will be like him yourself" (PROVERBS 26:4). *Lord, give me the patience to deal with people who speak in ignorance. Help me to get beyond my anger and lift them up in prayer. Guide my own thoughts, as well. Help me to learn about different cultures before I lock them into a narrow stereotype. Remind me that you've created us all in your image.*

PATRIOTIC

*May the God who gives endurance and encouragement give you a
spirit of unity among yourselves as you follow Christ Jesus, so that
with one heart and mouth you may glorify the God and Father
of our Lord Jesus Christ. Accept one another, just as Christ
accepted you, in order to bring praise to God.*

ROMANS 15:5–7

I WAS LEANING over the blue police barriers, waving my Puerto
Rican flag and waiting anxiously for the parade to begin. We
had been standing in the sun for two hours and, like any other nine-
year-old, I was restless for the festivities to begin. "When is it gonna
start?" I asked, twirling the flag like a baton. "My legs are tired."

My mother glared at me. "Very soon!" she replied for the fifth
time. My sister tapped me on the head with her flag. "Stop com-
plaining! If we hadn't come here early, we'd be back there," she said,
pointing to the large crowd of people behind us.

Before I could respond, I heard salsa music in the distance. "It's starting, it's starting!" I screamed. I wasn't the only one excited. People started pushing in for a better view and others began standing in front of the barrier. Surprisingly, the cops didn't ask them to leave. Instead, they moved another barrier in front of them and pushed the crowd back.

"Excuse me, Officer," my mother said, barely audible above the noisy crowd. "We were here first."

The officer moved on without responding as the music and crowd grew louder and louder. The first float had arrived, but all I could see were specks of color over the heads of the people in front of me. My mother tried to move us ahead of those who knowingly blocked our view, but no one budged. I didn't say a word. I just looked at my mother as she tried to fix the situation, without success. I held her hand tightly in this wild forest of bodies who were waving the same flag I'd been waving just minutes before.

"Forget it!" she yelled. "Let's go. We're going home." She had brought us here to celebrate our culture, but instead I felt anger toward the people who shared my nationality and had pushed us out of the way.

As a teenager, I went to the parade for the second time. The crowd was as intense as the first time, but my friends and I were determined to enjoy ourselves. I saw bits and pieces as we stretched our necks, stood on our toes, and walked around to catch a better view. What stood out for me this time were the guys who felt free to reach out and touch our hair or arms as we passed. "You got a number, baby?" they'd ask, staring us down and biting their bottom lip.

After that, I gave up attending the parade. Thirteen years later, in the process of writing this book, my editor urged me to go once more. "You have to go," she said, amazed that I hadn't already planned to attend. "The parade should definitely be one of your entries."

So off I went on a Sunday afternoon, following a river of people wearing Puerto Rican shirts, flags, and hats as they worked their way to Fifth Avenue. Despite being a bit late, I found a good spot, where I had a decent view of the floats and marchers. There were little girls in pageant gowns, smiling with painted lips and waving with excitement. Others, wearing long ruffled skirts and flowers in their hair, danced with a natural-born rhythm to the music. Kids were all over the place, playing instruments, twirling batons, and just enjoying their part in the parade. Seeing those beautiful children allowed me to focus on the pure innocence of pride that day, untainted by my past experiences.

It had always been difficult to find something that represented my own pride amid the general celebration of Puerto Rico each June—the larger-than-life flags draped on honking cars, the miniature flags painted on glossy fingernails, and the shouts of *"Boriqua."* That just wasn't the way I expressed my pride. Now I was looking into the bright faces of children celebrating our rich heritage with their wonderful talents, and nothing else mattered. We all shared the same pride, regardless of how we expressed it. I can testify, in my own way, that there's certainly a lot to be proud of.

Prayer

Lord, there are so many ways one celebrates pride and culture, just as there are many ways one celebrates love for you. There are congregations that shout and dance, while others praise in quiet meditation. Regardless of our style, you are the source of our worship. Unite us with one mouth and one mind as we lift up praises to you.

BROOKLYN SUMMERS

He turned the desert into pools of water
and the parched ground into flowing springs . . .

PSALM 107:35

ON A SCORCHING summer afternoon in Brooklyn, people surround the *piragua* man with their dollar bills. He takes his silver scraper, which looks like a toy truck, and shaves the top of the large ice block. Small slivers of refreshing ice shower the crowd as people wait their turn in the heavy sun. He empties the ice bits into a plastic cup, then pours on the bright syrup until this once-pale cup of ice is drenched in its sweet color.

A small girl sips the cherry juice from the top of her *piragua* as she waits for him to finish another for her grandfather. "*Gracias,*" she says, smiling with red-stained lips as she gives him the money. She crosses the street and hands her grandfather the cold cup with sticky pineapple-juice hands. "*Gracias, mamita,*" he says, giving her a gentle kiss on the forehead.

He puts the *piragua* next to his dominoes, which are lined up side by side like eager soldiers. The old men wait silently for the man with the straw hat to make his move, and with a hearty laugh, he smacks his domino down on the wooden table. A chorus of groans bellows from the competitors as they tip their game pieces over in defeat. The dominoes click and clack as they're flipped over and shuffled for the next game.

A teenage boy races down the front steps, past the old men, holding up a wrench in his hands as if it were an Olympic torch. Children wearing bathing suits and plastic flip-flops are waiting by the red fire hydrant, and they cheer when they see him. With a few strong turns on the hydrant nozzle, a gush of water jets onto the street. The teenager puts the wrench down on the concrete sidewalk, then picks up an empty tin can opened on both sides. He fits it over the rushing stream and tilts it upward, creating an enormous fountain. The children run underneath it, playing and spinning beneath the cool drops of water.

A driver taps his horn, sending them to the sidewalk like a flock of ducklings. The heavy drops tap on his roof, sounding like a bongo, as the children trickle back onto the street. He drives past a family packing their station wagon and stops for a moment to say hi. They're filling the back with blankets, towels, coolers, and huge pots of *arroz con gandules* and fried chicken for their beach picnic in Coney Island. They squeeze in, shut the doors, and drive off toward the waves—just another way to cool off on a hot, muggy summer day in Brooklyn.

Prayer

As the deer pants for streams of water, so my soul pants for you, O God. My soul thirsts for God, for the living God . . ." (PSALM 42:1, 2). *Lord, continue to satisfy my thirst for you. Fill me with your living water, that I may be used as a spring of refreshment in the communities of my church, my family, my work, and my neighborhood.*

MAMI

Love is patient, love is kind. It does not envy, it does not boast,
it is not proud. It is not rude, it is not selfseeking, it is not easily
angered, it keeps no record of wrongs. Love does not delight in evil
but rejoices with the truth. It always protects, always trusts,
always hopes, always perseveres.

1 Corinthians 13:4–7

F ORTY EUROS!" I shouted. "Are you serious?" The deliveryman
stood outside my little apartment in France, holding my
mother's package of "cute little shirts" she told me she'd send. "I'm
sorry, mademoiselle," he said. "It's the international shipping tax."

I was working part-time in France, teaching English, and the
small monthly paycheck left me on a ridiculously tight budget.
Forty Euros was a small fortune, but this man was holding my
mother's gift hostage until I paid up. I could see her distinct hand-
writing in bold ink—"Karen Valentin"—and I could picture her

folding each shirt with care and then sealing the package on the kitchen table.

International tax! I'd never heard of such a thing. Was this guy just trying to rip me off? Could I afford to hand over forty Euros and still get by the rest of the week? None of that mattered. I couldn't let him take it away. I wrote the check, which felt like a ransom payment, and snatched the box from his hands.

I couldn't stop crying as I opened the package on my bed and held the colorful new shirts in my hands. It had been months since I'd seen my family, and having a stranger almost deny me my mother's love offering made me feel even farther from home. In that moment, I felt such intense love and appreciation for her, I ached. This was just one token of my mother's free and selfless love, the same love that would scream out my name in delight when I'd call long-distance, even though we'd sometimes speak three times a week. It was the same love that made her deposit money into my account, even when I tried to pretend my finances were just fine.

As I put the shirts away in my closet, I thought about my mother's love and wondered what I'd ever done to deserve it. All I could remember were the things I'd done to push her away. When I was growing up, she used to call me "the lawyer" because I always had an answer and an argument for everything. Unlike my sister, who always asked first, I didn't wait for permission for a second ear piercing, to go out with friends, or to do anything else I thought she'd say no to. There was so much stubborn tension between us—especially in my teens—that I sometimes wished I didn't have a mother. I always seemed to focus on the traits that bothered me or perhaps mirrored my own flaws too vividly—the nervous habits, the careless forgetfulness, or the reluctance to stand up to people.

Through God's grace, our relationship healed as I grew older. There was less anger between us, but we still have our moments. She's quick to point out my shortcomings, but she never lets a day go by without an encouraging word, a compliment, or a loving phrase. I don't ever have to wonder if she's proud of me or seek her approval, because she always shows it. If you visit her home, she'll probably show you my oil paintings from high school and sit you down to listen to my demo CD. She'll most likely cry when she hears her favorites, even though she's heard them more times than anyone else. Afterward she'll go into a rant about me wasting my talent. "Such beautiful songs, and she hasn't done anything with it! She never finishes anything!"

All my life, she has been my biggest fan and my biggest rival—a complicated love that probably exists for many mothers and daughters. Regardless of our ups and downs, I'm so grateful that God chose this particular woman to be my mother.

That evening when I had dinner with friends, I wore one of the new shirts. I could almost feel her embrace in the fabric.

"Cute shirt!" my friend commented as I took off my coat.

"Thank you." I smiled. "I love it, too. It's a gift from my mother."

Prayer

Lord, thank you for mothers who love their children unconditionally. Help me honor those around me with love and respect, even in the midst of disagreement. No relationship is without problems, but I thank you for being the kind of God who heals old wounds and makes a way for new beginnings.

Desires of Your Heart

May he give you the desire of your heart
and make all your plans succeed.

PSALM 20:4

As I walked through the gym doors, the gymnasts who were running in a wide circle changed their direction and ran straight toward me. "Karen!" they screamed, their smiles as bright as their colorful leotards. They huddled around me with kisses and hugs as I looked at their faces in disbelief. "I can't believe how big you all are!" I kept repeating as I shook my head. For years, I'd watched them grow; yet given the short nine months I'd been away, their transformation seemed dramatic.

They ran back to the mat, excited to finish warm-ups and show me what they'd learned in my absence. How strange it felt to sit there and watch them as a visitor and not their coach. For ten years, that had been my life—spotting backflips, dragging heavy mats across the gym, and counting an endless number of push-ups and sit-ups. My new identity, as I sat in that familiar place, shocked me as much as seeing that my girls had grown so much. Things had changed in such a small amount of time that I almost didn't recognize myself.

Just under two years ago, in that very gym, I'd reached the height of discouragement and frustration with my life. It was my senior year at the university, and the only certainty in my future was the hefty student loan I had to pay back. Enthusiasm for coaching had faded long ago, and my talents and desires seemed unreachable as realistic career goals. The hope and optimism I'd once had about living out my dreams faded into the reality of "This is my life." The girls with their beautiful smiles would jump around the gym, bundles of energy and potential, while my own future seemed bleak and unpromising.

I settled into acceptance mode, believing God had answered my many tearful prayers with a no—but that's when He decided to shake things up in my life. After graduation, I was given an opportunity to teach English in France for nine months. Once there, God opened doors for me to visit many other European countries, fulfilling my desire for travel and my passion for languages. Before I left for Europe, I met a woman in a Bible-study group who encouraged me to write professionally and helped me put a book proposal together. When I was in France, I almost popped a blood vessel while screaming in disbelief as I checked my E-mail. Doubleday was giving me a contract to write my first book! It felt as if God had collected all my prayers until He had enough of them to sprinkle blessings over my head like confetti.

As I sat in the gym, it was hard to imagine the heaviness I had felt not so long ago. I had come full circle after this journey of unexpected blessings and felt reborn. I spent that afternoon watching the girls flip around, flying in the air with a weightless freedom. For the first time in a long time, I could relate.

Prayer

Father, you have heard my prayers, and I thank you. Continue to fulfill the desires of my heart, and take away those desires that don't flow with the plans you have for my future. Most of all, give me the patience to wait on your timing. I love you, Lord, and thank you for the abundance of your blessings.

GLOSSARY

arroz con gandules: rice with pigeon peas
bendito: an expression of compassion
bodega: a small grocery store/deli
boriqua: a Puerto Rican
casa: house
campo: the country
chancletas: slippers
chichon: bump on the body
coritos: short songs
de aquí: from here
doña: a title of respect for a woman
flaco: skinny

gloria a Dios: glory to God

gracias: thank you

hermanas: sisters

hermanos: brothers

la marqueta: a marketplace—usually located in a large open space where vendors sell produce and fresh meat from individual stands; term is a cross between the English word *market* and the Spanish word *mercado*

locos: crazy people

mamita: little mother (a term of endearment used to address females, both young and old)

mira: look

muslos: thighs

parranda: Christmas caroling—home-invasion-style, with family and friends

páseme una falda: pass me a skirt

pasteles: a meal comprised of pork, olives, and potatoes tucked in a bed of mashed green bananas, wrapped in wax paper, and boiled to consistency

piragua: snowcone

pobre flaco: poor skinny guy

pollo: chicken

que niña saludable: what a healthy child

rápido corren los carros cargados de azucar en el ferrocarril: fast run the cars loaded with sugar on the railway (a tongue twister for the Spanish double *rr* sound)

sangano: a foolish and ignorant person (may also denote laziness and freeloading)

te alabaré mi Dios: I praise you, my Lord

tilo: linden tree root

tio: uncle

vamos a hablar Español: let's speak Spanish